T0339767

NIETZSCHE

PHILOSOPHER OF
THE PERILOUS PERHAPS

NIETZSCHE

PHILOSOPHER OF
THE PERILOUS PERHAPS

Rebekah Peery

Algora Publishing
New York

Library of Congress Cataloging-in-Publication Data —

Peery, Rebekah S.
   Nietzsche, philosopher of the perilous perhaps / Rebekah S. Peery.
      p. cm.
   Includes bibliographical references (p.   ) and index.
   ISBN 978-0-87586-642-0 (trade paper: alk. paper)—ISBN 978-0-87586-643-7
(case laminate: alk. paper)—ISBN 978-0-87586-644-4 (ebook) 1. Nietzsche,
Friedrich Wilhelm, 1844-1900. 2. Power (Philosophy) 3. Christianity—
Philosophy. I. Title.

   B3318.P68P44 2008
   193—dc22

                                    2008030286

Front Cover:

Printed in the United States

TABLE OF CONTENTS

Foreword

It was a subject of interest and of serious, if limited, consideration by a few thinkers before him, as well as several others after him — "it" referring to "power" and "him" referring to the German philosopher, Friedrich Nietzsche. For him, writing in the latter half of the nineteenth century, it increasingly became the dominant principle, or concern, of his entire body of critical thought. He finally opened wide the door, and dared others to enter. He expected, anticipated, that in the future his followers, or at least some of them, would ultimately explore and further extend what he had begun.

Nietzsche understood well the dangers of daring to exercise his own enormous powers in investigating, and attempting to understand, what is probably the most complex phenomenon in man's world — *power*. He, no doubt, would recognize and proclaim the dangers of not daring to risk the dangers of such a task.

Influenced significantly by certain of the Pre-Socratics, Nietzsche was searching for a single unifying explanatory principle of the natural universe, one which would expressly allow the focus to be on human creatures. What he discovered was power. In my view, of all previous or present attempts, Nietzsche's thinking, and rethinking of power offers by far the most fertile ground for carrying the investigation forward. He was surely the architect, one might say the genius, who supplied the infrastructure for future developers.

Nietzsche realized early in his career that his major intellectual creative endeavor actually was, or would be, a destructive endeavor also. He made clear that his energies and abilities had ultimately been directed toward exposing the corrupting nature and power of Christianity in Western culture. In fact, he was matching his power against that of this religion. In his view, the devastating effects of the cultural force of Christianity were evident, spreading and growing. He believed that he was engaging in his own version of an apocalyptic, cosmic struggle, and that his involvement was, in his words, his "destiny."

Nietzsche was sufficiently wise and clever to realize also that this enterprise would be difficult, complicated, and especially hazardous. His perception of the significance of the threat that he was posing to the structural foundation of his own Western culture, and his keen awareness of the perilous position in which he was choosing to place himself, resulted in the necessity of disguise and of protection. His "deep thinking" required a "mask," or "masks." He would need to encourage misunderstanding, at least for a time. Perhaps until his life was finished, his intentions had to be concealed, made indistinct or imperceptible. His challenge was of such magnitude that it carried him far beyond atheism, infidelity, heresy, or blasphemy. My book "unmasks" Nietzsche as he surreptitiously and cleverly proceeded to expose the destructive power of Christianity on Western culture.

In addition to his choosing the use of a mask, or masks — with the suggestion that "contrariety might be the only proper disguise" — Nietzsche reminds us that he is particularly fond of conundrums, riddles, and puzzles. Concealed by his mask, his problems and solutions become puzzles and responses — interpretations, conjectures, guesses, experiments — further concealing and complicating access to the meaning of his threat.

The first part of the book develops a new interpretation of Nietzsche's devastating assault on Christianity, as he was constantly reminded of the difficulties posed by the mask and puzzles. Although the subject of my interpretation is Christianity, I focus, or refocus, attention on sexuality, or what I refer to as "gender-consciousness." Nietzsche's discussions of male and female, woman and man, the feminine and masculine, are not peripheral or incidental, but rather are central to his ultimate savage critique of Christianity. What might be called "sexual politics," meaning "the use of intrigue and stratagem to achieve a position of power," according to Nietzsche, had its origin with the arrival of Christianity, and had continued to be sustained, reinforced, and enhanced for two thousand years.

My reconsideration of Nietzsche's treatment of Christianity revealed the necessity of rethinking the importance of language, of power, and of values. I was drawn to the prospects of new or different ways of understanding these issues — not language, power, or values in the abstract, but as fundamental ever-present issues in the human culture.

Of no small significance is the issue of timing. Nietzsche clearly believed that he, his thinking, and his writing were "untimely," that perhaps he was among those who are "born posthumously." The transformations taking place within European culture in the latter part of the nineteenth century were seemingly abrupt, radical, and momentous. For him, these changes were evidence of the continuing deterioration and degradation of Western culture. Having been building for centuries, the source of this deterioration was identified with Christianity, especially its values, specifically its moral values. Nietzsche's "long perspective," his prescience, led him to his sense of urgency regarding the future, of the inevitability of a developing crisis. He spoke of "convulsions," "earthquakes," a crescendo of critical proportions. I might add the metaphor of "hurricane." He saw seeds, signs, warning signals — gaining in momentum, more intense and widespread, irreversible, heading inevitably toward some kind of catastrophe. His understanding of the changes occurring was based on his own experiences. Martin Heidegger said that Nietzsche felt the need "to scream."

What I suggest in this book is that we need to bring Friedrich Nietzsche back into the contemporary dialogue, to see and hear him with new and fresh ears and eyes, to listen again. Regardless of his tremendous influence and the continuing generation of critical interpretations of his writings, the use and misuse of his ideas, there remains a yet unrecognized and unexamined wealth of insights. It is time to bring Nietzsche into the rapidly growing turbulence characterizing so much of the contemporary discussions regarding religion, sexuality, power, values, and more. In my book I bring a new interpretation that weaves together the many strands that shaped his final assault on Christianity.

Nietzsche's interests in religion and power seem to have evolved simultaneously. This reciprocal relation between these two ideas meant that each was drawing on, and creating, energy and further understanding of both. This dynamic generated, and revealed the significance of, many of his other important ideas.

Nietzsche's focus on Christianity was one, as has been noted, of immediacy, of urgency, and the first part of my book is recognizing this imperative. The exercising of his energy and ability in exposing the dangers of religion revealed, at the same time, the more comprehensive nature of power. The second part of the book is intending to analyze and interpret the primary elements of the infrastructure enabling us to go further in understanding the phenomenon of power. One might call these the "postulates of power." All of these major ideas were developing together, "sprouting new shoots," overlapping, demanding to be recognized.

Just this brief reminder regarding Nietzsche's thinking. It was, and is, considered as revolutionary. As a "scientific philosopher," he radically interpreted all of the major areas of traditional philosophy — epistemology, or ideas regarding knowledge and the methods for securing it; ethics, or questions concerning the nature and sources of value, rightness, duty, and related matters; and metaphysics, or speculative inquiry concerning philosophical matters which are beyond the range of empirical inquiry. All of these underwent transformations of such magnitude that philosophical inquiry would never be the same. Nor would many of the newly emerging sciences or the arts. The cultural jolts are continuing to be felt.

As a classical philologist also, Nietzsche's studies familiarized him with the words of historians, philosophers, poets, and dramatists. His interests and research focused especially on the so-called "Pre-Socratics," and later extended back to mythological literature, as we will see. But here is the place to be reminded of three of the Pre-Socratics who appeared to catch his fancy, and more than his fancy. What he heard from these earliest philosophers must surely have aroused his curiosity and fascination in such a way, and to such an extent, as to be germinal in the development of his own philosophy.

Such a very few words of these earliest philosophers remain extant that they are usually referred to as "fragments." Here are a few. Empedocles claimed that the universe is eternal; that it consists of four elements — air, earth, fire, and water — in constantly changing patterns, these alternating between two forces, Love and Strife.

The ideas of Democritus, as we have them, are slightly more complex. He advanced the idea of change, or motion, requiring space which he thought of as a "void." The essential, defining nature of the world was "atoms in motion in a void." He thought about the smallest, indivisible material particles of which the universe is composed. Inherent properties of atoms, he speculated, were size, shape, and solidity. As to any other qualities, Democritus held that they were subjective, relative to the experiencing organism. Interestingly, he is attributed with the admonition, "The wise man limits his ambition according to his ability."

The third of these early philosophers of nature, the one who appears to have captivated Nietzsche's imagination most, was Heraclitus. According to Heraclitus, the universe is best understood as what he called "Logos," meaning something like the controlling principle of the universe, and translated variously as word, order, discourse, pattern, rationale, reason, and more. The Logos, or Word, is revealed as opposites, pairs which are unified by interdependence, but which exist in a state of constant strife. His reference symbolically to fire carried the meaning that everything in the universe is involved in an eternal process of change and exchange.

About a sixth of the extant fragments of Heraclitus deal with "opposites." They show four senses in which opposites are familiar. Considering the enormous influence of this thinking on Nietzsche, these are worth noting before we consider his own ways of developing them. First, Heraclitus wrote, "Over those who step into the same river, different and again different waters flow." Or, "Beginning and end are common on the circumference of a circle." Apparent paradoxes? Heraclitus was calling attention to one special sense of opposites — same and different. Second is polar opposition. "They would not know the name of Justice if the things [injustices] did not exist." "Sickness makes health pleasant and good; hunger, satiety; weariness, rest." Third is another kind of polar opposition that consists in the regular succession by one thing of its opposite, so that if one perished, so would the other. "The cold things get hot, hot gets cold, wet gets dry, parched gets damp." Or, the alternation between night and day, or sun and moon, and numerous others. Fourth, many oppositions are "subjective," dependent on the point of view, the nature, or the interests of the observer. "Swine rejoice in filth." "Sea is the cleanest and the dirtiest water: for fish it is drinkable, but for men it is undrinkable and poisonous." "The way up and down is one and the same," reflecting whether one lives in the valley or on the hill.

It is important to note that Heraclitus was not denying the existence of opposition. On the contrary, oppositions do exist, they do oppose; and the conflict of opposites is the basic fact of existence — according to Heraclitus. In his interpretation, not material "stuff," or substance, was most fundamental about the universe, but rather the continuing process of change. He added that failure to understand this "Logos," or rationale, was the source of all evil.

Eternal motion, change, process, and especially Heraclitus' emphasis on the notion of opposition — all became essential elements in Nietzsche's thinking. But Heraclitus had made thinking itself the process — the continuing process, involving constant change and exchange. And of course, speaking and writing, the "stuff" in this case being words.

In spite of his skepticism and often satirical comments concerning the classical philosophers — Socrates, Plato, and Aristotle — Nietzsche recognized the significance of their application of the ideas which these earlier three philosophers had made. They were continuing, and extending, the dialectical process of opposites to man, rather than the earlier focus on natural processes. Socrates introduced the ideas of questions and answers, the continuing change and exchange of views that might lead to further knowledge, to more understanding. The power residing in this approach was apparent.

Plato, of course, took the focus on words — on questions and answers, on conversation, on the process of thinking, on motion involved in change and exchange of ideas — to the level of his famous Dialogues. Aristotle took his own turn toward thinking, and the use of many words, into comprehensive, lengthy analysis and interpretation.

Nietzsche, as philosopher and philologist, as cultural critic and historian, became fully aware of the significance and power of ideas and words, in the constant and continuing motion and conflict of speaking. He recognized and celebrated his own increasing energy and ability in using words, in expressing power. And we now recognize and celebrate, and are awed by that power.

This book is separated into three parts. The first part investigates Nietzsche's exercise and expression of power as he confronted the power of Christianity. This conflict was the major one in which he observed and learned, becoming wiser regarding the complexities of the nature and dynamics of power. It had the urgency of a "command performance" for him.

The second part of the book engages in the task of examining and extending our understanding of the phenomenon of power, with fully acclaiming the creative genius of Nietzsche in giving us the elements upon which to build.

The third part of the book changes the focus back to Nietzsche, considering four different perspectives. We look at him as "the experimenter," "the contrarian," "the historian," and "the revolutionary."

PART ONE

CHAPTER I. DANGERS, PUZZLES, AND MASKS

In the October 8, 2006 issue of *The New York Times Book Review*, these words appear:

> Friedrich Nietzsche may be the most exciting philosopher — ever! Not just because he is obviously so smart. Not just because he writes so beautifully. Not just because of his peculiar ideas and themes and topics. But because Nietzsche forces us to think and rethink more than anyone else in the modern Western tradition.
>
> Nietzsche provokes us. He teases us. He seduces us. Nietzsche changes lives. And it is this lonely, frantic, self-styled prophet who flips the switch into the tumultuous 20th century.

A "scientific" philosopher, yes. But also a classical philologist, a physiological psychologist, a poet, a cultural historian and critic, and more. But perhaps most, a *thinker*. About himself, Nietzsche says he is not a saint, not a prophet, not an improver-of-mankind, not a preacher, not a moral monster, not a fanatic — but yes, perhaps, a buffoon, and certainly an experimenter. And an immoralist. And, of course, a disciple of the philosopher Dionysos. Not to overlook Heraclitus, the philosopher of change and opposition.

There is more. Nietzsche was aware that he was an "untimely" man with "untimely" thoughts and words. "Thoughts out of season." He wrote:

Every deep thinker fears being understood more than he fears being misunderstood . His vanity may suffer from the latter, but his heart, his fellow-feeling suffers from the former. *(BGE, 230)*

And he adds, "You see, I do my best to be understood with difficulty." Nietzsche leaves little doubt as to his desire, his need, to conceal his thoughts and words, perhaps to be understood at some later "timely" time. As he said, "Some are born posthumously." He believed the unbelievable, thought the unthinkable, spoke and wrote the unspeakable. He was aware of himself and his words as dangerous. A friend, Peter Gast, commenting to Nietzsche concerning the title of one of Nietzsche's last books, *Twilight of the Idols,* wrote:

> [Y]ou have driven your artillery on the highest mountain, you have such guns as have never yet existed, and you need only shoot blindly to inspire terror all around. . . . *(PN, 464)*

Nietzsche himself wrote, "The Germans invented gunpowder — all credit to them! But they made up for it by inventing the printing press." Nietzsche's words were dynamite. In *Twilight of the Idols* he wrote:

> Great men, like great ages, are explosives in which a tremendous force is stored up; their precondition is always historically and physiologically, that for a long time much has been gathered, stored up, saved up, and conserved for them — that there has been no explosion for a long time. Once the tension in the man has become too great, then the most accidental stimulus suffices to summon into the world the "genius," the "deed," the great destiny. What does the environment matter, then, or the age, or the "spirit of the age," or "public opinion"! *(PN, 547)*

And what about the "genius"?

> There are two types of genius: one which above all impregnates and wants to impregnate; another which likes to be impregnated and gives birth. . . . These two types seek each other like man and wife, but they also misunderstand each other — like man and wife. *(BGE, 184)*

In what were some of his last words to himself, about himself, and to his perhaps future disciples and interpreters, in his book *Ecce Homo,* Nietzsche wrote:

> I know my fate. One day there will be associated with my name the recollection of something frightful — of a crisis like no other before on earth, of the profoundest collision of conscience, of a decision evoked *against* everything that until then had been believed in, demanded, sanctified. I am not a man. I am dynamite.
> — . . . I was the first to *discover* the truth, in that I was the first

to sense — smell the lie as lie. . . . My genius is in my nostrils. . . . For when truth steps into battle with the lie of millennia we shall have convulsions, an earthquake spasm, a transposition of valley and mountain such as has never been dreamed of. The concept politics has then become completely absorbed into a war of spirits, all the power-structures of the old society have been blown into the air — they one and all reposed on the lie: there will be wars such as there have never yet been on earth. Only after me will there be grand politics on earth. (*EH*, 126, 127)

He had become aware that he was a "time-bomb." "Living dangerously," which for Nietzsche meant thinking and writing dangerously, meant at the same time, that he needed to develop a *style* suitable to meet his requirements that he be misunderstood and also understood. There is little doubt that his unique style contributes as much to the undiminished power of his words to excite, provoke, tease and perplex as to the possibility of understanding the extraordinary explosive nature of his thoughts. As he remarked, "I don't think thoughts, thoughts think me." So, in the early pages of his *Beyond Good and Evil*, he teasingly wrote:

Everything deep loves masks; the deepest things have a veritable hatred of image and likeness. Might not *contrariety* be the only proper disguise to clothe the modesty of a god? A question worth asking. It would be surprising if some mystic hadn't at some time ventured upon it. There are events of such delicate nature that one would do well to bury them in gruffness and make them unrecognizable. . . . Such a concealed one, who instinctively uses speech for silence and withholding, and whose excuses for not communicating are inexhaustible, *wants* and encourages a mask of himself to wander about in the hearts and minds of his friends. And if he doesn't want it, one day his eyes will be opened to the fact that the mask is there anyway, and that it is good so. Every deep thinker needs a mask; even more, around every deep thinker a mask constantly grows, thanks to the continually wrong, i.e., superficial, interpretations of his every word, his every step, his every sign of life. — (*BGE*, 46, 47)

Perhaps Nietzsche is reaffirming the importance of the notion of the Pre-Socratics that the world is primarily characterized by the interplay of opposite forces. Perhaps recalling Aristotle's "law of contradiction." Or even the use of Aquinas' "on the contrary." In any case, contrariety suggests something contrary, or of opposite nature, character, direction or position. Opposite, contrary, or reverse imply that two things differ from each other in such a way as to indicate a definite kind of *rela-*

tionship. Opposite suggests symmetrical antithesis in position; contrary sometimes adds to opposite the idea of antagonism. Some of the contraries of particular interest and significance for Nietzsche are appearance and reality, change and permanence, beginning and end, descent and ascent, same and different, under and over, higher and lower, up and down, soft and hard, excess and defect, light and heavy, affirmation and denial, sun and moon, belief and disbelief, sickness and health, truth and untruth, male and female. And perhaps most important for his project of revealing while concealing these incendiary thoughts are the contraries *playful* and *serious.* The heaviest subjects often needed the lightest touch. In this he is unsurpassable. Words for him were *tools, toys,* and *weapons.*

In conversing with Nietzsche expect to hear puns, metaphors, similes, aphorisms, poetry, analogies, *double entendres,* myths, fables, legends, parodies, parables, oxymorons, symbols, conundrums, puzzles, irony, ellipses, allegories and riddles. All of these in a mixture with, and ultimately in service to, those deep thoughts.

During Nietzsche's active life, 1844–1888, as he reminds the reader, only forty-four years, Europe was experiencing new heights in the renaissance of culture. The cultural awakening taking place in science or the sciences, in philosophy, and in the arts was reaching new levels, greater possibly than anything previously known to the human community. Nietzsche's situation, his experiences, in this environment must have engulfed him, overwhelmed him. But part of his life experiences included also familiarity with earlier forms, for example, fictitious forms such as fables, often with animals, or inanimate things as speakers or actors designed to teach a moral (Aesop, Leonardo). In Nietzsche's evaluation of his own writings, *Thus Spoke Zarathustra* was his greatest work, a special gift to mankind. *Zarathustra* — an imaginative work, a fable which begins with the eagle and serpent and ends with the dove and the lion. Or other fictitious forms — legends, unhistorical or unverifiable stories, handed down by tradition from earlier times, popularly accepted as historical. Also myths, one of a class of stories, usually concerning gods, semi-divine heroes, etc., current since primitive times, the purpose of which is usually the attempt to explain some belief or natural phenomenon, some power or powers (myth of

Demeter, Zeus). Nietzsche called himself a "god" and a disciple of the god Dionysus.

The changes, the transformations, taking place within European culture seemingly were abrupt, rapid, radical, momentous — perhaps beyond evolutionary to revolutionary. At the same time, correlating with these external changes, the "internal" changes for Nietzsche appear to have been extraordinary. As he suggested, "thoughts think me," "metaphors rush to my attention," or "puns offer themselves in abundance." Many of these thoughts were like bullets, piercing, painful, and potentially "life-threatening." He needed, perhaps, a "life-jacket," a "steel helmet." To diminish the possibility of danger or pain to others, he would cover these harsh "truths" in ways such that they might "taste" better. That meant to make use of his creative genius — his imagination and his natural talent for humor, for wit, for laughter. Along with that natural talent for seriousness.

Take the metaphor — a figure of speech in which a term, or phrase, is applied to something to which it is not literally applicable, in order to suggest a *resemblance*. For example, "a mighty fortress is our God," or Nietzsche's "Supposing that Truth is a woman" — . Or consider the pun — the humorous use of a word or phrase so as to emphasize or suggest its different meanings or applications, or the use of words that are alike or nearly alike, or nearly alike in sound but different in meaning. The puzzle and the riddle were favorites of Nietzsche's. A puzzle — something baffling, confusing, perplexing, testing or requiring ingenuity. A riddle is a puzzle, intentionally obscure, with magical effects, solved by guessing. Riddle, as a symbol, may mean "untying a knot," "a hatching egg," "the strain of sprouting seed," "the birth of a child." Nietzsche and Nietzsche's Zarathustra are drunk, not on alcohol, but "riddle drunk." Scientists, former philosophers, and perhaps theologians, solve problems, Nietzsche solves puzzles and riddles. And equally important, he creates puzzles and riddles. The world, nature, life, the body are mysterious, filled with ambiguity. Approaching Nietzsche, a reader must be willing to play his word games.

In the commotion and excitement of the constant barrage of thoughts, these thoughts, and the words to express them, seem to have arrived in many sizes, randomly, often vague (like Hegel's "notions"), unfinished, competing with other thoughts for attention. The result is everything from ellipses, or aphorisms, to the full-length *Zarathustra*. Nietzsche said, "I would rather say in ten words what others might say in a book — or might not say in a book."

In addition to paying attention to his *style* or styles, it is important to listen to the *tone* of his words. Early in the evolution of his thinking he spoke softly, quietly. During the process the tone hardened, until in his latest writing he seems to have felt the need to scream. He wrote, "They all talk about me but no one gives me a thought." No one was listening, and consequently no one could understand and speak about his "truth." Again, "Must one smash their ears before they learn to listen with their eyes?" And finally, all of Nietzsche's thinking and speaking is *personal*, very personal. But such is the case with every thinker, every speaker, every writer.

A further bit of intrigue may be achieved by noting the titles of some of his books, or "chapters," or "headings," etc. For example: *Untimely Meditations*, *The Dawn*, followed later in his life by *The Gay Science*, *Beyond Good and Evil*, *Twilight of the Idols*, *The Antichrist*, and of course, *Ecce Homo*. Not ordinary titles. Read the 383 titles of separate short essays in *The Gay Science*. Or the 80 titles of the speeches of *Zarathustra*. Of similar interest are the titles which he gives to the nine "Articles" in *Beyond Good and Evil*. Most attention drawing, however, are a few of the chapter titles in his "autobiography." Speaking to himself, and perhaps to a few selected readers — "Why I Am So Wise," "Why I Am So Clever," "Why I Write Such Good Books," and "Why I Am A Destiny."

So, suppose that we consider Nietzsche's thinking and writing as a *puzzle*, or *riddle*, or *mystery* — as baffling, confusing, perplexing — testing or requiring our ingenuity. We should assume that there are clues, evidence that might lead to a possible solution. At the same time, consider that his ideas — flamboyant, extravagant, curious, or strange — are a treasure, a collection of great worth or value, seemingly inexhaustible.

During his relatively short but intense creative life, a few notions, or ideas, appear to have increasingly captured the attention and imagination of thinkers and writers of different persuasions, including Nietzsche. Among these was the idea of *experience* — everything that is perceived, understood, remembered, both external and internal, e.g.

passions, the feeling of power. There was growing awareness that experiences, although always individual and unique, took two similar but different forms — female and male. These differences in experiences reflected the physiological differences regarding female and male bodies. The awareness of these differences began early in the development of Nietzsche's thinking and increased dramatically throughout his writing career. Very early he wrote:

> When one speaks of *humanity*, the idea is fundamental that this is something which separates and distinguishes man from nature. In reality, however there is no such separation: "natural" qualities and those called truly "human" are inseparately grown together. Man, in his highest and noblest capacities, is wholly nature and embodies its uncanny dual character. (*PN*, 32)

The "uncanny dual character" of all living things in nature — *female* and *male*.

Closely connected to the idea of experience, for Nietzsche, was that of *phenomenon* — any fact, event, situation, external or internal, usually involving the senses, was to be considered a phenomenon. Nietzsche once suggested that the only thing present immediately and directly in experience might be the passions.

Another closely related major idea, with expanding present and possible future significance, was the idea of *consciousness*; that is, acute awareness of, interest in, concern with, especially one's own experience or experiences. This interest in consciousness quickly expanded into species consciousness, class consciousness, race consciousness, gender or sexual consciousness, national consciousness, and historical or time consciousness. This usually included the growing awareness of, interest in, concern with one's own biological, or social or economic *rank* in society, a feeling of identification with those belonging to the same group or class as oneself.

Charles Darwin's theory relating to species consciousness and Karl Marx's theory relating to class consciousness, along with the interest of both in historical consciousness — historical development or historical evolution — were already beginning to shake the traditional foundations of the West, especially the Christian religious base. Nietzsche was not unaware of the potential for conflict that each of these modes of consciousness entails. His own emerging or evolving concern, however, was not (primarily, at least) with species, class, race, or nationality, but rather with sexual or gender consciousness and with historical consciousness, as the latter opened up new possibilities for understanding the former.

We should take note of these additional ideas. *Evolution, revolution, scientific method,* and *experimentation* appear to have emerged and loomed large in the consciousness of most of the major creative and imaginative figures of the times, evolution meaning a process of gradual, relatively peaceful change usually from a lower, simpler or worse state to a more complex, better or higher state, and revolution signifying sudden, radical or pervasive change, usually in political organization or in society and the social structure. For Nietzsche everything seemed to be about the process of *change,* both evolutionary and revolutionary. His own sense and embrace of change was more threatening. He was seeking fundamental change in the way of thinking about or visualizing something, a change of paradigm, sweeping reversals. There can be little doubt of the enormous influence on Nietzsche of evolutionary thinking and thinkers. However, it is difficult to dispute that he was increasingly becoming a revolutionary thinker with enormous uncalculated power. It has been suggested that his ideas and words were evolving during his entire productive life. At the same time, they were being formed into the earth-shaking revolution of which he was very conscious.

Mention should be made of another sense of revolution which appears increasingly as Nietzsche's thinking developed. That is, to revolve, to rotate, or to recur, to return in succession, as of the seasons, or night and day. He seems to have been persuaded in favor of a cyclic interpretation of history, contrary to the more accepted view in his own time, of history as a linear progression. One of his own major well-debated ideas was that of *eternal recurrence.* Later we will consider in more detail the impact of such a view of history on his thinking.

As Nietzsche's own body and his life were evolving, his consciousness was evolving, his *self*-consciousness. He clearly was expressing his increasing awareness of himself as an individual, as a male individual, as a male *body,* similar to other male bodies. Also evolving was his gender or sexual consciousness, his awareness of the physiological differences between male and female bodies, and of the possible psychological and social implications of those differences. Part of his own genius, and of his distress, was that his consciousness — species, race, class, nationality, gender, historical — was racing far ahead of those of his contemporaries.

We might take another perspective on some of the influences on Nietzsche's thinking, on his reading, and on who may have influenced him. He said that his recreation was reading books. He was a classical philologist and became something of a "philologist of Christianity." He knew the Bible. He discovered the writings of the German philosopher, Arthur Schopenhauer, at an early age and "became" a philosopher. He appears to have been especially attracted to the so-called Pre-Socratics and to have been well-read in the classical, as well as modern, philosophers. He was fond of Ralph Waldo Emerson. At the age of twenty-four he wrote to a friend, Franz Overbeck:

> [M]y mother read to me: Gogol, Lermontov, Bret Harte, M. Twain, E. A. Poe. If you do not yet know the latest book by Twain, *The Adventures of Tom Sawyer,* it would be a pleasure for me to make you a little present of it. . . . (PN, 73)

It has been noted that Sigmund Freud said of Nietzsche that he probably understood himself better than any man who had ever lived. Probably correct. It could be said also that he probably read more extensively and deeply than any man before him.

Nietzsche was born in the parsonage of his father, who was the village pastor and the son of a pastor. His mother was the daughter of a pastor of a nearby village, only eighteen years of age at the time of Nietzsche's birth. His father died when Nietzsche was five years of age. The family now consisted of Nietzsche, his paternal grandmother, his mother, his sister Elizabeth (two years his junior) and two maiden aunts. During his life he had many men friends of whom he spoke and with whom he often corresponded. He was also — to quote one of his biographers — "highly sexed and inordinately attracted to women. . . . He had many women friends, but not one wife or mistress."

Throughout his writing career Nietzsche constantly brought up the subjects of man and woman. This "uncanny dual character" of nature, as he called it, this female–male duality, was a constant theme. And any possible understanding of Nietzsche's thinking would require recognizing its significance. When he wrote, "I know woman," he drew on a wealth of experience. But regarding many things he had to say concerning woman, he added, "I assume that everyone now understands how much these truths are only — *my* truths. — "

So again, let's not approach Nietzsche's thinking/writing as if he were treating his concerns as a typical philosopher. Instead, we will consider him as he considered himself — as a puzzler, a riddler, mysterious. Constantly searching for clues, an analogy seems to offer possibilities — that of a *rope*. Rope — a large stout cord of strands twisted or braided together. The strength of the rope requires the strength of each strand or fiber. Each strand needs to be examined separately as carefully as possible, before trying to figure out the possible intricate patterns of overlapping strands or themes. One additional note —symbolically rope has been taken to represent divine power. Or back to the notion of having a puzzle to try to solve — Nietzsche's puzzle, or puzzles. How does one go about trying to solve a crossword puzzle, or a jigsaw puzzle? Try a word here, or a small piece of a very large design. Experiment, possibly relate each word or piece to others. It's often painstaking. And so we will find this puzzle.

Chapter 2. Power and Value

Many of Nietzsche's thoughts about *power* are known to his readers, and power seems to present itself as probably the most fruitful starting point. But before looking into some of his own views, it may be helpful to recall that two of Nietzsche's predecessors, both of whom were apparently familiar to him, had written extensively on the subject of power — Niccolo Machiavelli and Thomas Hobbes. It is not difficult to suppose that especially Hobbes may have influenced Nietzsche's thinking. Hobbes' greatest work, the *Leviathan*, appeared in 1651. Usually he is referred to as having developed a philosophy of naturalism and the first major philosophy of power. Here are a few noteworthy excerpts:

> So that, in the first place, I put for a general inclination of all mankind a perpetual and restless desire of power after power that ceases only in death. And the cause of this is not always that a man hopes for a more intensive delight than he has already attained to, or that he cannot be content with a moderate power, but because he cannot assure the power and means to live well which he has present without the acquisition of more. And from thence it is that kings, whose power is greatest, turn their endeavors to the assuring it at home by laws or abroad by wars; and when that is done there succeeds a new desire — in some, of fame from new conquest; in others, of ease and sensual pleasure; in others of admiration or being flattered for excellence in some art or other ability of the mind. (*AE*, 179)

Hobbes says further:

> The power of a man, to take it universally, is his present means to obtain some future apparent good; and is either *original* or *instrumental*. *Natural power* is the eminence of the faculties of body or mind, as extraordinary strength, form, prudence, arts, eloquence, liberality, nobility. *Instrumental* are those powers which, acquired by these or by fortune, are means and instruments to acquire more, as riches, reputation, friends, and the secret working of God, which men call good luck. For the nature of power is in this point like to fame, increasing as it proceeds; or like the motion of heavy bodies, which the further they go, make still the more haste. (*AE*, 178)

A third quotation may have been particularly significant for Nietzsche, as we will see later. Hobbes wrote:

> The *value* or worth of a man is, as of all other things, his price — that is to say, so much as would be given for the use of his power — and therefore is not absolute but a thing dependent on the need and judgment of another. An able conductor of soldiers is of great price in time of war present or imminent, but in peace not so.... A learned and incorrupt judge is much worth in time of peace, but not so much in war. And as in other things so in men, not the seller but the buyer determines the price. For let a man as most men do, rate themselves at the highest value they can, yet their true value is no more than it is esteemed by others.... *Worthiness* is a thing different from the worth or value of a man, and also from his merit or desert, and consists in a particular power or ability.... (*AE*, 178, 179)

As far as I am aware, Hobbes was the first philosopher to explicitly and in detail connect *power* and *value*, a relationship of critical importance for Nietzsche, as we will see later.

Nietzsche would also have championed Hobbes' belief that ideas, and by extension words, are more dangerous, i.e., more powerful than actions. And finally, Hobbes is famous for his appraisal of life in the so-called "state of nature" — "and the life of man, solitary, poor, nasty, brutish, and short." Nietzsche's own thinking about *life* remains for later.

For both Machiavelli and Hobbes, their analyses, or interpretations, of power were focused on political power, the power of the state, the ruler, or the institutions of government. Nietzsche recognizes political and economic power, but his interests and perspectives, his interpretations, involved a much larger range — one might say, global. Especially, as we will see, he fully recognized the awesome power of religion and religious institutions, particularly Christianity.

Before hearing Nietzsche's own words, perhaps a valuable beginning would be to review the various meanings, or expressions, which attach to the idea or word "power." These are important — energy, ability, capability, capacity, strength, influence, might, force, inspire, persuade, arouse, authority, dominate, control, and command. *Capability* suggests the potential or ability to act, produce, generate, create (and destroy). *Authority* suggests the power to rule, to direct the actions or thoughts of others, usually because of *rank*, to issue commands and punish violations. *Control* suggests power or influence applied to complete or successfully complete, regarding persons or actions — usually implying the requirement of fear, weakness or obedience. *Influence* suggests personal and unofficial power derived from deference of others to one's character, ability or rank — the power to arouse, inspire, excite, incite, persuade, impress, directly affect opinions, ideas, taste. Nietzsche had the *power* — the energy, the ability, to destroy and create ideas and *words*, to *influence* others.

And now on to Nietzsche and power. He might have said, "In the beginning was the Word, and the word was power. . . ." and that the ancients created many gods and goddesses to represent that power, or those powers. But let's begin here:

> And do you know what "the world" is to me? Shall I show it to you in my mirror? This world: a monster of energy, without beginning, without end; an immovable, brazen enormity of energy, which does not grow bigger or smaller, which does not expend itself but only transforms itself; as a whole of unalterable size, a household without expenses or losses, but likewise without increase or income; enclosed by "nothingness" as by a boundary; not something flowing away or squandering itself, not something endlessly extended, but as a definite quantity of energy set in a definite space and not a space that might be "empty" here or there, but rather as energy throughout, as a play of energies and waves of energy at the same time one and many, increasing here and at the same time decreasing there; a sea of energies flowing and rushing together, eternally moving, eternally flooding back, with tremendous years of recurrence, with an ebb and flow of its forms; out of the simplest forms striving towards the most complex, out of the stillest, most rigid, coldest form towards the hottest, most turbulent, most self-contradictory, and then out of this abundance returning home to the simple, out of the play

of contradiction back to the joy of unison, still affirming itself in the uniformity of its courses and its years, blessing itself as that which must return eternally, as a becoming that knows no repletion, no satiety, no weariness — : this is my *Dionysian* world of the eternally self-creative, the eternally self-destructive, this mystery world of the twofold delight, this my "beyond good and evil," without aim, unless the joy of the circle is itself an aim; without will, unless a ring feeling goodwill towards itself — do you want a *name* for this world? A *solution* for all your riddles? A *light* for you too, you best concealed, strongest, least dismayed, most midnight men? — *This world is the will to power — and nothing beside!* And you yourself are also this will to power — and nothing beside! (*N*, 136)

Nietzsche perceives and interprets "the world" as a "monster of energy" and *names* it "the will to power." And in some sense that opens up an endless array of his attempts to elaborate on this idea. This may be an appropriate place to include Nietzsche's thoughts concerning names, or naming. Early in his thinking he wrote:

> *Only as creators!* — This has given me the greatest trouble and still does: to realize that what things *are called* is incomparably more important than what they are. The reputation, name, and appearance, the usual measure and weight of a thing, what it counts for — originally almost always wrong and arbitrary, thrown over things like a dress and altogether foreign to their nature and even to their skin — all this grows from generation unto generation, merely because people believe in it, until it gradually grows to be part of the thing and turns into its very body. What at first was appearance becomes in the end, almost invariably, the essence and is effective as such. How foolish it would be to suppose that one only needs to point out this origin and this misty shroud of delusion in order to *destroy* the world that counts for real, so-called "*reality*." We can destroy only as creators. — But let us not forget this either: it is enough to create new names and estimations and probabilities in order to create in the long run new "things." (*BGE*, 121, 122)

Later we will find how important this notion of *naming* becomes for Nietzsche. It also became a significant possible way of understanding names for several of his successors, notably Jean-Paul Sartre and Maurice Merleau-Ponty, the latter recognizing the "power of signifying speech."

While Nietzsche was developing his doctrine of the will to power, he wrote:

> *On the doctrine of the feeling of power.* — Benefiting and hurting others are ways of exercising one's power over others; that is all one de-

sires in such cases. One hurts those whom one wants to feel one's power, for pain is a much more efficient means to that end than pleasure; pain always raises the question about its origin while pleasure is inclined to stop with itself without looking back. . . . Certainly the state in which we hurt others is rarely as agreeable, in an unadulterated way, as that in which we benefit others; it is a sign that we are still lacking power, or it shows a sense of frustration in the face of this poverty; it is accompanied by new dangers and uncertainties for what power we do possess, and clouds our horizon with the prospect of revenge, scorn, punishment and failure. (*GS, 86,* 87)

Nietzsche is suggesting here that hurting others is a sign that one lacks power — something of a contrary position from conventional belief. Creating or destroying are ways of exercising one's power, enhancing or diminishing life, affirming or denying one's own fate, and especially destroying old values and creating new ones. Regarding *values*, Nietzsche wrote:

We who think and feel at the same time are those who really continually *fashion* something that had not been there before: the whole eternally growing world of valuations, colors, accents, perspectives, scales, affirmations, and negations. . . . Whatever has value in our world does not have value in itself, according to its nature — nature is always value-less, but has been given value at some time, as a present — and it was *we* who gave and bestowed it. Only we have created the world *that concerns man!* But precisely this knowledge we lack, and when we occasionally catch it for a fleeting moment we always forget it again immediately; we fail to recognize our best power and underestimate ourselves, the contemplatives, just a little. We are *neither as proud nor as happy* as we might be. (*GS,* 241, 242)

The importance for Nietzsche of creating new "things" by creating new names, and the importance of creating values, cannot be overstated, and we will pursue these further later.

But more about power. R. J. Hollingdale, one of Nietzsche's best translators and critics, wrote this:

To grasp Nietzsche's theory of will to power and its ramifications one cannot do better than trace the idea as it appears at this or that place in his works and see how it formed into a hypothesis which was then consciously employed, consistently yet still experimentally, as an explanatory principle. (*N,* 76)

Hollingdale's brief discussion of Nietzsche's philosophy of power in his book entitled *Nietzsche* (Routledge Author Guides) is excellent, and as he says in his Preface, "Interpretation is ultimately no more than a necessary method of presentation: the book's objective is to make the reader want to read Nietzsche for himself. If it succeeds in that objective, the reader will quickly become his own 'interpreter'."

Nietzsche, by taking the idea of power "globally," so to speak, presented himself almost literally with endless opportunities, or perspectives, to suggest what that might mean. His attention remained focused within the natural world, the world of *nature*, as he perceived and reflected on it. For example, the energy exhibited by the four elements — air power, fire power, water power, and earth power. Or, the power of the five senses — seeing, hearing, tasting, smelling, touching.

For Nietzsche the vital force, the impulse to life, the "élan vital," that which he described as the basic nature of all living things, was this impulse or drive for power, what he called the "will to power." He believed it would be possible, and attempted to understand *all* human behavior by experimentally applying this idea to countless examples of human activity. His own rich experiences, personal and historical, were his evidence. Having power, the feeling of power, preserving and enhancing power, became in his thinking the sole motive for humans. The differences in behavior were a matter of means to the end — power. Only the means might be judged, not the end. A "common basic drive" unites the most diverse activities. This is the fundamental fact of life, for every living thing.

Human beings, persons and the extraordinary possible powers associated with human bodies — that was Nietzsche's focus. *Life*, the actual biological, physiological process of producing new life, more life; sexuality, the basic fact, the first premise, the presupposition of life — female and male bodies — the "uncanny duality of nature." The basic expression, or exercise, of the will to power is creativity, the power of generation — taken in its broadest sense. Beyond creating life, there is little doubt that Nietzsche most valued the thoughts, and the ability to communicate those thoughts in words, the power of speaking and writing — the *power of words*. In fact, to create and speak words about the physiological process of creating life — of all creating and generating.

Two additional important points may be made here, to be reconsidered again later. First, Nietzsche seems to agree with Hobbes that power is the standard of all *value*. In establishing what he refers to as a "table of values," it is *who* is valued, then *what actions* are valued, and then *what things* are valued. And recall, values are created by individuals. The second point concerns the question of *rank*, and Nietzsche writes:

> What determines rank, sets off rank, is only quanta of power, and nothing else. . . .

> Order of rank as order of power: war and danger the presupposition for a rank to retain the condition of its existence. . . . What determines your rank is the quantum of power you are: the rest is cowardice. (*WP*, 457)

Keep in mind that Nietzsche held strongly the belief that "Whatever has value in our world does not have value in itself, according to its nature — nature is always value-less, but has been given value at some time as a present — and it was we who gave and bestowed it. Only we have created the world *that concerns man!*" But most importantly, for Nietzsche we have created the values goodness, beauty, and truth. We have called things "good," "beautiful," or "true." And we have created, and continue to create or re-create, an order of rank among things; rank is never "in the world," so to speak. Philosophers and theologians, according to him, along with the militarists, have been the primary creators of orders of rank. Nietzsche does play with the word "rank" in suggesting that "my genius is in my nose — I smell 'rank'." More about this later.

Martin Heidegger, a devoted follower of Nietzsche, insisted that failure of any interpreter of Nietzsche to recognize the significance of the idea of *reversal* in his thinking would encounter extraordinary difficulty. And this may be the major instance. Purposes, meanings, names, but possibly most importantly, values are constantly in flux, never stable, constantly changing — never absolute, objective, permanent, eternal, or certain. Values, and primarily moral values, form the foundation, the basic structure of any human culture, the driving force of history. This thinking was truly revolutionary. The questions revolving around the issue of values had been at the top of Nietzsche's concerns from an early age. And as his thinking evolved, moral values, aesthetic values, and religious values drew most of his attention.

Near the beginning of one of his last works, *The Antichrist*, we find these questions and answers:

What is good? — All that heightens the feeling of power, the will to power, power itself in man. What is bad? — All that proceeds from weakness. What is happiness? — The feeling that power *increases* — that a resistance is overcome. (N, 76)

Speaking of these questions and answers, Hollingdale says:

The abruptness and uncompromisingness of these assertions are characteristic of the works of 1888: they are a condensation of the sense and purpose of the whole "philosophy of power" as it has been built up during the course of years. (N, 76)

There is little doubt that Nietzsche had reached his own interpretation that the possibility exists for a different exercise of power. Power over oneself, command of oneself, rather than over others. And the possibility of creating oneself, considering as he says, that we are both "creature" and "creator." Read a typical passage from *The Gay Science*:

One thing is needful. — To "give style" to one's character — a great and rare art! It is practiced by those who survey all the strengths and weaknesses of their nature and then fit them into an artistic plan until every one of them appears as art and reason and even weaknesses delight the eye. Here a large mass of second nature has been added; there a piece of original nature has been removed — both times through long practice and daily work at it. Here the ugly that could not be removed is concealed; there it has been reinterpreted and made sublime. Much that is vague and resisted shaping has been saved and exploited for distant views; it is meant to beckon toward the far and immeasurable. In the end, when the work is finished, it becomes evident how the constraint of a single taste governed and formed everything large and small. Whether this taste was good or bad is less important than one might suppose, if only it was a single taste! ... For one thing is needful: that a human being should attain satisfaction with himself, whether it be by means of this or that poetry and art; only then is a human being at all tolerable to behold. Whoever is dissatisfied with himself is continually ready for revenge, and we others will be his victims, if only by having to endure his ugly sight. For the sight of what is ugly makes one bad and gloomy. (GS, 232, 233)

We shall continue to explore the close connections between power and value. Who has value? Who creates, or has in the past, created values? And in the present and future? However, there is another major idea of Nietzsche's, equally revolutionary — *perspectivism*, as he understood it. He wrote:

[T]oday we are at least far from the ridiculous immodesty that would be involved in decreeing from our corner that perspectives are permitted only from this corner. Rather has the world become "infinite" for us all over again, inasmuch as we cannot reject the possibility that *it may include infinite interpretations. (GS, 336)*

Here the resounding notion that there are probably infinite perspectives, infinite interpretations of these perspectives, even "Alas, too many *ungodly* possibilities of interpretation. . . ." He even said of himself that he was able to "invert his perspectives." Important for later. Perspectivity, or perspectivism, it appears, is the basis of human life.

The importance for Nietzsche of the idea of *reversal* is reflected in his rejection of the dogmatic, or categorical, for the suppositious, or hypothetical; the absolute for the relative; the abstract for the concrete; the universal for the particular; the impersonal for the personal; of certainty for uncertainty or ambiguity. More concerning the application of this idea will emerge.

Chapter 3. Bachofen in Basel

Returning to the possible, or probable, influences on Nietzsche's thinking, particularly who may have had such a role, there is one person who remains in the shadows, so to speak. And it seems compelling that we pursue this lead. In the vast amount of critical literature that has been written regarding Nietzsche's thinking, the ideas of power and of value remain of major concern; his interest in sexuality less so. However, looming largest, most well-known — if not understood — and most controversial has been his exhausted, and apparently exhausting, notorious attack on religion, particularly Christianity. All of his numerous original and creative ideas seem to have coalesced to support this dangerous mission. Everything — his "fate" seemed to have been leading inexorably in this direction. It was, as he said many times, his "destiny."

We have mentioned that Nietzsche was born into and raised in a family of Lutheran pastors. It appears that in his teens he began to slowly move away from this familial religious environment. In his last work, *Ecce Homo, How One Becomes What One Is*, he says, "And so I tell myself my life." And a few pages later he writes:

> I have never reflected on questions that are none — I have not squandered myself. — I have, for example, no experience of actual religious difficulties. I am entirely at a loss to know to what

extent I ought to have felt "sinful." I likewise lack a reliable criterion of a pang of conscience: from what one *hears* of it, a pang of conscience does not seem to me anything respectable. . . . To honour to oneself something that went wrong all the more *because* it went wrong — that rather would accord with my morality. — "God," "immortality of the soul," "redemption," "the Beyond," all of them concepts to which I have given no attention and no time, not even as a child — perhaps I was never childish enough for it? — I have absolutely no knowledge of atheism as an outcome of reasoning, still less as an event: with me it is obvious by instinct. I am too inquisitive, too *questionable*, too high spirited to rest content with a crude answer. God is a crude answer, a piece of indelicacy against us thinkers — fundamentally even a crude *prohibition* to us: you shall not think! (*EH, 51*)

At the age of twenty Nietzsche entered Bonn University as a student of theology and classical philology. Later transferring to Leipzig, he read Schopenhauer, relinquished the Lutheran religion, became familiar with philosophical inquiry, and at Easter, at the age of twenty-one abandoned the study of theology and formally renounced his religion.

In 1967 a book entitled *Myth, Religion, and Mother Right,* Selected Writings of J. J. Bachofen, was published by Princeton University Press, in a series of works sponsored by the Bollingen Foundation, with a preface by George Boas and introduction by Joseph Campbell. In order to establish and support what appears to be an almost undeniable strong influence of Bachofen's thinking and writings on Nietzsche, what follows are several quotations from both Boas and Campbell, as well as direct quotations from the author, Bachofen. Boas begins the Preface:

> The name of Johann Jakob Bachofen, if mentioned at all in books of reference, is attached to a theory of social development which maintains that the first period of human history was matriarchal. And if any discussion of the theory is added, it will be to the effect that it is almost universally discredited. As a matter of fact this is only a small part of Bachofen's contribution to social philosophy, and it would be perhaps more appropriate, if labels are required, to list him among either ethnologists or sociologists. For, as the studies in this volume will show, his attitude toward cultural history was not that of the empirical anthropologist or that of the annalist. His focus of interest was the inner life of human beings rather than what he called the externals of human development. He was more concerned with literature, language, architecture, and the other arts than with economic factors, military adventures, territorial expansion, the succession of rulers,

population growth, and revolutions, whether in isolation from one another or all in a grand hodge-podge. (*MR*, xi)

Campbell begins the Introduction:

> It is fitting that the works of Johann Jacob Bachofen (1815–1887) should have been rediscovered for our century, not by historians or anthropologists, but by a circle of creative artists, psychologists, and literary men: . . . For Bachofen has a great deal to say to artists, writers, searchers of the psyche, and, in fact, anyone aware of the enigmatic influence of symbols in the structuring and moving of lives: the lives of individuals, nations, and those larger constellations of destiny, the civilizations that have come and gone. . . . (*MR*, xxv)

Further into the Introduction Campbell refers to Bachofen's "young friend Friedrich Nietzsche," and writes:

> Nietzsche, who came to Basel in 1869 as a young professor of classical philology and for the next half decade was a frequent guest in Bachofen's home (spending Sundays, however, with his idol Richard Wagner in Lucerne, whose dates, 1813–1883, again approximately match Bachofen's span of years), saw the dialectic of history, and of individual biography as well, in terms of an unrelenting conflict between the forces of disease, weakness, and life-resentment, on the one hand, and on the other, the courage and determination to build a life forward toward a realization of potentials. (*MR*, xlvi, xlvii)

A few paragraphs later Campbell writes:

> The arrival in Basel, three years later, of Nietzsche, brought a new brilliance to the Bachofen domestic circle, and it was about that time that signs began to appear, as well, of a new, significant, and rapidly increasing scientific appreciation of his published works — not, indeed, from the classical circles of academic hardshelled crabs to which he had turned, at first, in vain; but from the unforeseen quarters of a new science, anthropology. (*MR*, li)

Further, with reference to the relationship between Bachofen and Nietzsche, Boas writes:

> There are certain themes in Bachofen which have a strong similarity to those of Nietzsche. Though Bachofen's name does not appear in any of the indexes to any of Nietzsche's works, Nietzsche was a great admirer of Bachofen's colleague, Jakob Burckhardt, and Burckhardt himself was an admirer of Bachofen. . . . It is to be noted also that in his early *Birth of Tragedy* Nietzsche took over Bachofen's terms the Dionysiac and the Apollonian, for two types of will, the creative and the contemplative, and that he also maintained that they were fused into one in the Greek tragedy before the time of Euripides. (*MR*, xx)

Later, significant differences appear between Nietzsche's philosophy and that of Bachofen; however, one of the important similarities is that of the role assigned by both to symbols and myths. Bachofen himself speaks of "Dionysian truth" and "Dionysian religion." Even though, as Boas points out, Bachofen's name apparently does not appear in any of the indexes of Nietzsche's works, and although apparently no translator, biographer, or critic of Nietzsche's works has referred to his lengthy acquaintance with Bachofen, it is reasonable to assume that the young scholar would have had many absorbing and invigorating conversations with the older scholar. And equally reasonable to consider what possible influences Bachofen's thinking may have had on this young classical philologist.

In a short biographical sketch written by Bachofen (1815–1887) in 1854, he wrote:

> I was drawn to the study of law by philology. It is here that I started and hither that my legal studies led me back. In this respect my attitude toward my field has always remained unchanged. Roman law has always struck me as a branch of classical and particularly of Latin philology, hence as part of a vast field encompassing the whole of classical antiquity . . . it was ancient and not modern Roman law that I really wanted to study. (MR, 3)

Bachofen's interest was Latin philology; Nietzsche's interest was mainly Greek philology. As a jurist, Bachofen entered into the study of the history of Roman law. At the age of twenty-four, he began a series of trips, spending time in universities and museums in Paris and London. Of his stay in London he wrote, "I was fascinated by the life of the law courts with all their patriarchal pomp, but there was also the British Museum with its treasures."

Bachofen's literary studies led him, he writes, to "Winckelmann's History of Art." He continues:

> But to my reading of Winckelmann's works I owe an enjoyment of a far higher order — indeed, one of the greatest pleasures of my whole life. Since then I have dwelt much in the regions that it opened, especially at times when everything else seemed to lose interest for me. Ancient art draws our heart to classical antiquity, and jurisprudence our mind. Only together do the two confer a harmonious enjoyment and satisfy both halves of man's spirit. Philology without concern for the works of art remains a lifeless skeleton. . . . In my wanderings through the museums of Italy my attention was soon attracted to one aspect of all their vast trea-

sures, namely mortuary art, a field in which antiquity shows us some of its greatest beauties. When I consider the profound feeling, the human warmth that distinguishes this realm of ancient life, I am ashamed of the poverty and barrenness of the modern world. The ancient tombs have given us a well-nigh inexhaustible wealth. At first we may regard the study of tombs as a specialized field of archeology, but ultimately we find ourselves in the midst of a truly universal [religious] doctrine. All the treasures that fill our museums of ancient art were taken from tombs.... Antiquity made full use of the symbolic, most enduringly and profoundly in its art.... The sun warms and illuminates these resting places of the dead so wonderfully, and infuses the abodes of horror with the magic of joyous life. What beauty there must have been in an age whose very tombs can still arouse so much yearning for it! What a vast abundance of beautiful ethical ideas the ancients drew from their myths. The treasure house that encompasses their oldest memories of history serves also as a source of the oldest ethical truths, and provides consolation and hope for the dying. (MR, 10, 11, 12, 13)

More study, more reading, more trips to Italy and London and the British Museum, and he wrote:

Rome became the fulfillment and end of a cultural era spanning a millennium.... I found myself in a period of transition such as occurs in the life of every striving man.... Ever since then my guiding thought has been the religious foundation of all ancient thinking and life.... What I am engaged upon now is true study of nature. The material alone is my preceptor. It must first be assembled, then observed, and analyzed. (MR, 14, 15, 16)

Bachofen's learning, interests and experience — jurisprudence, history of Roman law, classical philology, symbolism and mythology — coalesced into what may be called "cultural history." He was interested not only in individual symbols or myths, or individual cultures, but in discovering what he called "the universal law of history," — in developing his theory of "scientific history." The development of his thinking reflected, and was consistent with, theoretical historical thinking of his time. The dominant ideas regarding history were first — history develops in discernable stages. Not to be understood as cause and effect, but rather as one stage containing the potential, or seeds, for the succeeding stage, with each stage taken up into the next stage. Second — that this development was unilinear, involving a series of changes, usually from primitive to more advanced, from simple or lower to more complex or higher, an ascending process. Third — that there were so-called "law" or "laws" which should be discoverable. Perhaps Bachofen might have referred to this "universal law of history" as a pattern, or patterns — as natural or chance configuration, repeatable or recurring again and again.

Later Nietzsche would reject the notion of a "law" or "laws" of nature, preferring instead the idea of "necessity" or "necessities," repeatable again and again, or "recurring eternally." In any case, in considering the evidence, the material to be "assembled, observed and analyzed" consisted of the symbols in art and the myths in literature. For symbols and myths, and their interpretations, were the source of understanding the meaning of life for the ancients. This meant a study of nature and what he referred to as "nature religions." Bachofen was persuaded that he, and we, needed and were able to have access to, pre-classical and pre-Christian culture and the religion. He wanted to study and learn from myths and symbols, but also from all available sources in classical literature, language, and the arts. To effectively develop his theory of the history of culture, he needed to be able to trace the development, the transformations, from these pre-classical, ancient cultures through various stages up to, and including, the present — the Christian era.

Before hearing further some of Bachofen's words, this may be noted. He perceived the fundamental duality of nature, and of life, as residing primarily in the opposition of male and female, and life and death, and in the constant conflict between these opposites. Sexuality, power or powers, both natural and "supernatural," values, rankings, attitudes, beliefs, behaviors — all of these were important considerations in Bachofen's interpretation of the history of culture. And he interpreted the highest force shaping cultures, the basic foundation of any culture, as being religion.

Bachofen's theory was one interpreting history as a linear progression from lower forms — which he calls "matriarchal, or maternal" — to higher forms — which he calls "patriarchal, or paternal." The most important principle operating as stimulus, or catalyst, for the emergence of a new and different stage was the intensification, abuse, or perversion of *power* by either the female/woman/mother or the male/man/father. Boas, in his Preface to Bachofen's writings reminds us, "Bachofen's theory of a matriarchal society out of which modern patriarchal societies evolved was accepted pretty generally among sociologists until about the beginning of the twentieth century. It was the classic pattern for historians to follow." As earlier in his life, once again however, Bachofen's interpretations were derided, dismissed, and virtually disappeared.

The details of his theory form the substance of his book *Myth, Religion, and Mother Right*. Here we can provide only a few of his words which serve mostly to indicate the basic themes of his attempt to describe five separate stages in this evolutionary process. Bachofen's own Introduction begins:

> The present work deals with a historical phenomenon which few have observed and no one has investigated in its full scope. Up until now archeologists have had nothing to say of mother right. The term is new and the family situation it designates unknown. The subject is extremely attractive, but it also raises great difficulties. The most elementary spadework remains to be done, for the cultural period to which mother right pertains has never been seriously studied. Thus we are entering upon virgin territory.
>
> We find ourselves carried back to times antedating classical antiquity, to an older world of ideas totally different from those with which we are familiar. . . . The matriarchal organization of the family seems strange in the light not only of modern but also of classical ideas. . . . The main purpose of the following pages is to set forth the moving principle of the matriarchal age, and to give its proper place in relationship both to the lower stages of development and to the higher levels of culture. . . . In this way I hope to restore the picture of a cultural stage which was overlaid or totally destroyed by the later development of the ancient world. . . . Polybius' passage about the matriarchal genealogy of the hundred noble families among the Epizephyrian Locrians suggests two further observations which have been confirmed in the course of our investigations: (1) mother right belongs to a cultural period preceding that of the patriarchal system; (2) it began to decline only with the victorious development of the paternal system. . . .
>
> The principles which we have deduced from a few observations are confirmed in the course of our investigation by an abundance of data. . . . The prestige of womanhood among these people was a source of astonishment to the ancients, and gives them all, regardless of individual coloration, a character of archaic sublimity that stands in striking contrast to Hellenic culture. (*MR*, 69, 70, 71)

A little later Bachofen writes:

> Both the mythical and the strictly historical traditions present very similar pictures of the system. Products of archaic and of

much later periods show such an astonishing accord that we almost forget the long interval between the times when they originated. . . . Precisely in regard to the most important aspect of history, namely, the knowledge of ancient ideas and institutions, the already shaky distinction between historic and prehistoric times loses its last shred of justification. (MR, 73)

Bachofen traces what he calls the "juridical aspect" of mother right, indicating that in matriarchal cultures the sister, daughter, and youngest child are found to have the favored position over the brother, son, or oldest child. Considering what he calls the "ethical aspect" he writes:

The ethical aspect strikes a resonance in a natural sentiment which is alien to no age: we understand it almost spontaneously. At the lowest, darkest stages of human existence the love between the mother and her offspring is the bright spot in life, the only light in the moral darkness, the only joy amid profound misery. By recalling this fact to our attention, the observations of still living peoples of other continents has clarified the mythical tradition which represents the appearance of the (father lovers) as an important turning point in the development of human culture. The close relation between child and father, the son's self-sacrifice for his begetter, require a far higher degree of moral development than mother love, that mysterious power which equally permeates all earthly creatures. Paternal love appears later. The relationship which stands at the origin of all culture, of every virtue, of every nobler aspect of existence, is that between mother and child; it operates in a world of violence as the divine principle of love, of union, of peace. Raising her young, the woman learns earlier than the man to extend her loving care beyond the limits of the ego to another creature and to direct whatever gift of invention she possesses to the preservation and improvement of this other's existence. Woman at this stage is the repository of all culture, of all benevolence, of all devotion, of all concern for the living and grief for the dead. (MR, 79)

Next Bachofen addresses the controversial question of the religious aspect of matriarchy:

The religious foundation of matriarchy discloses this system in its noblest forms, links it with the highest aspects of life, and gives a profound insight into the dignity of that primordial era which Hellenism excelled only in outward radiance, not in depth and loftiness of conception. . . . There is only one mighty lever of all civilizations, and that is religion. Every rise and every decline of human existence springs from a movement that originates in this supreme sphere. Without it no aspect of ancient life is intelligible, and earliest times in particular remain an impenetrable riddle. Wholly dominated by its faith, mankind in this stage links every form of existence, every historical tradition, to the basic religious idea, sees every event in a religious light, and identifies itself completely with its gods. If especially matriarchate must bear this hieratic imprint, it is because of the essential feminine nature, that profound sense of the divine presence which, merging with the feeling of love, lends woman, and particularly the mother, a religious devotion that is most active in the most barbarous times. The elevation of woman over man arouses our amazement most especially by its contradiction to the relation of physical strength. The law of nature confers the scepter of power on the stronger. If it is torn away from him by feebler hands, other aspects of human nature must have been at work, deeper powers must have made their influence felt. . . . The religious primacy of motherhood leads to a primacy of the mortal woman; Demeter's exclusive bond with Kore leads to the no less exclusive relation between mother and daughter; and finally, the inner link between the mystery and the chthonian-feminine cults leads to the priesthood of the mother, who here achieves the highest degree of religious consecration.

These considerations bring new insight into the cultural stage characterized by matriarchy. We are faced with the essential greatness of the pre-Hellenic culture: in the Demetrian mystery and the religious and civil primacy of womanhood it possessed the seed of noble achievement which was suppressed and often destroyed by later developments. . . . But mystery is the true essence of every religion, and wherever woman dominates religion or life, she will cultivate the mysterious. Mystery is rooted in her very nature, with its close alliance between the material and the supersensory; mystery springs from her kinship with material nature, . . . Hellenism is hostile to such a world. The primacy of motherhood vanishes, and its consequences with it. The patriarchal development stresses a completely different aspect of human nature, which is reflected in entirely different social forms and ideas. (*MR*, 84, 85, 87, 89)

Bachofen continues:

The central idea that I have emphasized from the outset, the relationship between the primacy of women and the pre-Hellenic culture and religion, is eminently confirmed by the very phenomena which, when viewed superficially and out of context, seem to argue most against it. Wherever the older mystery religion is preserved or revived, woman emerges from the obscurity and servitude to which she was condemned amid the splendor of Ionian Greece and restored to all her pristine dignity. . . . No era has attached so much importance to outward form, to the sanctity of the body, and so little to the inner spiritual factor . . . and none has been so given to lyrical enthusiasm, this eminently feminine sentiment, rooted in the feeling of nature. In a word, matriarchal existence is regulated naturalism, its thinking is material, its development predominantly physical. Mother right is just as essential to this cultural stage as it is alien and unintelligible to the era of patriarchy. (*MR*, 90, 92)

Having made his case for the significance of mythology and for the necessity of attempting to interpret and understand these earliest forms of human culture; and having devoted an enormous amount of research to understanding the inner structure of the matriarchal system, especially assigning to religion the dominant position in that system, Bachofen next turned his attention to history, to determine the relation of the matriarchal culture to other cultural stages. He writes:

> We shall come face to face with a new aspect of history. We shall encounter great transformations and upheavals which will throw a new light on the vicissitudes of human destiny. Every change in the relation between the sexes is attended by bloody events; peaceful and gradual change is far less frequent than violent upheavals. Carried to the extreme, every principle leads to the victory of its opposite; even abuse becomes a lever of progress; supreme triumph is the beginning of defeat. Nowhere is man's tendency to exceed the measure, his inability to sustain an unnatural level, so evident; and nowhere is the scholar's capacity for entering into the wild grandeur of crude but gifted peoples, and for making himself at home among utterly strange ideas and social forms, put to so rigorous a test. . . . But it is precisely the connection of the sexual relationship and the lower or higher interpretation with the totality of life and the destinies of nations that relates our study directly to the cardinal questions of history. (MR, 92, 93, 99)

Bachofen's investigations led him to speak at length regarding what he called the "Dionysian religion." Here, briefly is one important excerpt:

> The magic power with which the phallic lord of exuberant natural life revolutionized the world of women is manifested in phenomena which surpass the limits of our experience and our imagination. Yet to relegate them to the realm of poetic invention would betoken little knowledge of the dark depths of human nature and failure to understand the power of a religion that satisfied sensual as well as transcendent needs. It would mean to ignore the emotional character of woman, which so indissolubly combines immanent and transcendent elements, as well as the overpowering magic of nature in the luxuriant south.

> Throughout its development the Dionysian cult preserved the character it had when it first entered into history. With its sensuality and emphasis on sexual love, it presented a marked affinity to the feminine nature, and its appeal was primarily to women; it was among women that it found its most loyal supporters, its most assiduous servants, and their enthusiasm was the foundation of its power. Dionysus is a woman's god in the truest sense of the word, the source of all woman's sensual and transcendent

hopes, the center of her whole existence. It was to women that he was first revealed in his glory, and it was women who propagated his cult and brought about its triumph. A religion which based even its higher hopes on the fulfillment of the sexual commandment, which established the closest bond between the beatitude of supersensory existence and the satisfaction of the senses, could not fail, through the erotic tendency it introduced into the life of women, to undermine the Demetrian morality and ultimately to reduce the matriarchal existence to an Aphroditean hetaerism patterned after the full spontaneity of natural life. . . . All life was molded by the same trend, as is shown above all by the ancient tombs which, in a moving paradox, became the chief source of our culture of the erotic sensuality of Dionysian womanhood. Once again we recognize the profound influence of religion on the development of all culture. The Dionysian cult brought antiquity the highest development of a thoroughly Aphroditean civilization, and lent it that radiance which overshadows all the refinement and all the art of modern life. (*MR*, 101, 102)

Later in the book he writes this:

The progress from the maternal to the paternal conception of man forms the most important turning point in the history of the relations between the sexes. The Demetrian and the Aphroditean-hetaeric stages both hold to the primacy of generative motherhood, and it is only the greater or lesser purity of its interpretation that distinguishes the two forms of existence. But with the transition to the paternal system occurs a change in fundamental principle; the older conception is wholly surpassed. An entirely new attitude makes itself felt. The mother's connection with the child is based on a material relationship, it is accessible to sense perception and remains always a natural truth. But the father as begetter presents an entirely different aspect. Standing in no visible relation to the child, he can never, even in the marital relation, cast off a certain fictive character. Belonging to the offspring only through the mediation of the mother, he always appears as the remote potency. As promoting cause, he discloses an immateriality over against which the sheltering and nourishing mother appears as (matter), as (place and house of generation), as (nurse). (*MR*, 109)

Bachofen ends his Introduction with these words:

The present book makes no other claim than to provide the scholarly world with a new and well-nigh inexhaustible material for thought. If it has the power to stimulate, it will gladly content itself with the modest position of a preparatory work, and cheerfully accept the common fate of all first attempts, namely to be disparaged by posterity and judged only on the basis of its shortcomings. (*MR*, 120)

Chapter 4. Myths and Symbols

It would be difficult to over-estimate the probable influences on Nietzsche's life and career from this long acquaintance between these two imaginative, creative, revolutionary thinkers. Both set out to radically change the human world by changing our understanding of that world. Bachofen, the elder, bequeathed to Nietzsche, the younger, in the latter's early, formative, and impressionable years, a treasure — a mother lode — of energy, power, excitement, possibilities. Nietzsche's obvious natural talent for, and love of, ideas and words to express those ideas, and his awareness of the power of words, must have been stimulated beyond any anticipations. Words to learn more about the past, to understand the present, and to help shape the future — these were the aims of both. Nietzsche frequently sounds as if he is on a high, giddy, drunk with possibilities. He came to believe that not only are perspectives and interpretations unlimited, but even more generally, possibilities of many sorts were unlimited. I believe he was overwhelmed, perhaps terrified, as to where his possibilities, his ideas and words, might take him. The tensions of his short active life appear to have been a constant struggle between the relentless pulling toward, and resistance to, new ways of perceiving the world, nature, life, humans.

These are the themes in Bachofen's legacy that seem to stand out. First — the notion of a scientific approach to understanding history, particularly cultural history, with his focus on language, literature, architecture, and other arts. Second — the emphasis on the idea that the key element of cultural history was the study of nature, the continuing changes in the male–female relationship, between the feminine principle and the masculine principle, the maternal and the paternal, sexuality, the centrality and the sanctity of the body. Third — the interpretation of the power and force of religion as having first rank among the creative forces of culture, as the foundation of culture. Fourth — the necessity of recognizing that the language of myths and symbols was the key to understanding the earliest stages of the process of cultural history. Myths and symbols provided reliable evidence for early thinking regarding the natural primal relation, that of the sexes, and also regarding questions of life and death, of generating life and destroying life, and more.

I am suggesting that we now can see what would be most of the basic ingredients which continued to perplex and drive Nietzsche's thinking throughout his life. Science or scientific method, art, history, religion, sexuality or sexual politics, as well as power or powers, values, perspectivism, and language or words. Given Nietzsche's insistence on the ambiguity of nature, as well as of ideas and words, it would seem that Bachofen's emphasis on myths, and especially on symbols, added immeasurably to Nietzsche's awareness of the unlimited power potential of words. New dimensions, new modes, new possibilities to speak both directly and indirectly about those "very dangerous and deep truths." His delight is palpable. He is able to draw on symbols to create his puzzles, to have fun as he is addressing the most serious of questions, to take at times a light approach to the heaviest of problems. And he appears especially to have been reminded and intrigued that symbols frequently arise in pairs, as opposites — suggesting that "uncanny dual character of nature." And he became further aware that many pairs of symbols have historically been used in representing the basic opposites — male and female. One last observation from Bachofen reads:

> This homogeneity of matriarchal ideas is confirmed by the favoring of the left side over the right side. The left side belongs to the passive feminine principle, the right side to the active masculine

principle. The role played by the left hand of Isis in matriarchal Egypt suffices to make the connection clear. But a multitude of additional data prove its importance, universality, primordiality, and freedom from the influence of philosophical speculation. Customs and practices of civil and religious life, peculiarities of clothing and headdress, and certain linguistic usages reveal the same idea. . . . Another no less significant manifestation of the same basic law is the primacy of the night over the day which issued from its womb. . . . Already the ancients identified the primacy of the night with that of the left, and both of these with the primacy of the mother. And here, too, age-old customs, the reckoning of time according to nights, the choice of the night as a time for battle, for taking counsel, for meting out justice, and for practicing the cult rites, show that we are not dealing with abstract philosophical ideas of later origin, but with the reality of an original mode of life. . . . Extension of the same idea permits us to recognize the religious preference given to the moon over the sun, of the conceiving earth over the fecundating sea, . . . (MR, 77)

Nietzsche recognized the inexhaustible opportunities in symbolic opposites and seized these opportunities, both to re-explore traditional opposites and to create and experiment with new ones of his own — most in the service of speaking about female and male, woman and man. Recall an earlier quotation:

Everything deep loves masks; the deepest things have a veritable hatred of image and likeness. Might not *contrariety* be the only proper disguise to clothe the modesty of a god? A question worth asking. It would be surprising if some mystic hadn't at some time ventured upon it. (*BGE*, 46)

Perhaps a few examples will serve to further convince Nietzsche's reader of his cleverness and his wit, especially with symbols. In recounting the events which had led to his writing of the book which he considered his greatest, *Thus Spoke Zarathustra, A Book for Everyone and No One*, he recalls the enterprise which began in 1881 and ended in 1883. "[T]he pregnancy is seen to have lasted eighteen months. This term of precisely eighteen months might suggest, at least to Buddhists, that I am really a female elephant." He adds this:

The text, I may state expressly because a misunderstanding exists about it, is not by me: it is the astonishing inspiration of a young Russian lady with whom I was then friendly, Fraulein Lou von Salome. (*EH*, 100)

In describing the type of character which is his Zarathustra, Nietzsche writes:

> He contradicts with every word, this most affirmative of all spirits; all are in him bound together in a new unity. . . . It is precisely this compass of space, in this access to opposites that Zarathustra feels himself to be the *highest species of all existing things.* . . . (EH, 106, 107)

In "Zarathustra's Prologue," at the beginning of the book, in addressing the sun, Zarathustra spoke:

> For ten years you have climbed to my cave: you would have tired of your light and of the journey had it not been for me and my eagle and serpent. (Z, 9)

It would be difficult to find two richer symbols than that of the eagle and that of the serpent — both symbols of energy or power. Only to say here that the eagle symbolizes the male principle, the father, and is associated with the gods of power and war. As for the serpent, there appears to be a clear connection between the snake and the feminine principle, the mother, and is associated with the Mother Goddess — to refer to the most primitive strata of life. Zarathustra ends his long adventures in the company of his doves and lion — again, both having a great variety of symbolic meaning, almost always associated with power and generation. Perhaps this long book may be considered Nietzsche's fable, in contradiction to what he considered the fable of Christianity.

Also, from *Zarathustra* is this more familiar exchange:

> "Why so hard?" the kitchen coal once said to the diamond. "After all, are we not close kin?" Why so soft? O my brothers, thus I ask you: are you not after all my brothers?
>
> Why so soft, so pliant and yielding? Why is there so much denial, self-denial, in your hearts? So little destiny in your eyes?
>
> And if you do not want to be destinies and inexorable ones, how can you one day triumph with me?
>
> And if your hardness does not wish to flash and cut and cut through, how can you one day create with me?
>
> For creators are hard. And it must seem blessedness to you to impress your hand on millennia as on wax.

Blessedness to write on the will of millennia as on bronze — harder than bronze, nobler than bronze. Only the noblest is altogether hard.

This new tablet, O my brothers, I place over you: *become hard!* (*Z*, 214)

Hard and soft, male and female? Perhaps, future creators of a new "tablet of values," the "revaluation of all values" which became increasingly important for Nietzsche.

Finally, consider this teaser. Nietzsche's Preface to his *Beyond Good and Evil* begins:

Supposing that Truth is a woman — well, now is there not some foundation for suspecting that all philosophers, insofar as they were dogmatists, have not known how to handle women? That all the gruesome earnestness, the left-handed obtrusiveness, with which they have usually approached Truth have been unskilled and unseemly methods for prejudicing a woman (of all people!) in their favor? One thing is certain: she has not been so prejudiced. (*BGE*, xi)

CHAPTER 5. CHRISTIANITY AND CULTURE

It is hardly arguable that Nietzsche's notoriety is most often associated with his perspectives on, and his interpretations of, religion — that is, Christianity. His thoughts and words on the subject began very early and continued to gain in momentum, scope, and intensity until his last words were recorded: " — Have I been understood? — *Dionysos against the Crucified.* . . . " All of his other major interests, it appears, were mustered into the service of his ultimately devastating and ruthless critique. From almost wondering mildly and softly, to his coming to an awareness that no one was able to hear him, by the time he wrote *The Antichrist*, one of his last books, all the restraints were off. He was, in fact, screaming.

Early on, Nietzsche was perceiving and describing Western culture as descending, deteriorating, dying, decadent, decomposing. And he began to concern himself with the ways, if possible, of interrupting or reversing this condition. He was in agreement with Bachofen's interpretation which viewed religion as the primary creative force shaping culture, the foundation of any culture. If this were so, then it meant that the responsibility for such degradation was to be found in Christianity, and the charges made were numerous. New and dangerous questions were necessary.

As with much of Nietzsche's thinking, one can follow fairly closely, though imperfectly, the evolution or development of that thinking concerning religion. We know of the religious environment of his childhood and youth, and of his rejection of the profession of theology in favor of classical philology. And we have learned of the apparent influence of his long acquaintance with Bachofen. Nietzsche was aware of the impact and triumph of Darwin's theory of evolution and of the increasing challenges to Christianity by the new theories of science. His introduction to philosophy was his discovery of Schopenhauer, the first major openly philosophical atheist, and also perhaps incidentally, an ardent misogynist.

Nietzsche's earliest perspectives and musings on Western, especially German, culture were more in the form of reporting on what appeared to be growing obvious challenges to the idea of God. In *Human, All Too Human,* he wrote:

> *Christianity as antiquity.* When we hear the old bells ringing out on Sunday morning, we ask ourselves can it be possible? This is for a Jew, crucified two thousand years ago, who said he was the son of God. The proof of such a claim is wanting.
>
> Within our times the Christian religion is surely an antiquity jutting out from a far-distant olden time; and the fact that people believe such a claim (while they are otherwise so strict in testing assertions) is perhaps the oldest part of this heritage. A god who conceives children with a mortal woman; a wise man who calls upon us to work no more, to judge no more, but to heed the signs of the imminent apocalypse; a justice that accepts the innocent man as a proxy sacrifice; someone who has his disciples drink his blood; prayers for miraculous interventions; sins against a god, atoned for by a god; fear of the afterlife, to which death is the gate; the figure of the cross as a symbol in a time that no longer knows the purpose and shame of the cross — how horribly all this wafts over us, as from the grave of the ancient past! Are we to believe that such things are still believed? (*HA*, 84, 85)

A few years later in *The Gay Science* we find these words:

> *Against Christianity.* — What is now decisive against Christianity is our taste, no longer our reasons. (*GS*, 186)

And these:

> *Changed taste.* — The change in general taste is more powerful than that of opinions. Opinions, along with all proofs, refutations, and the whole intellectual masquerade, are merely symptoms of the

change in taste and most certainly not what they are still often supposed to be, its causes. (*GS*, 106)

And these:

> Above all, one should not wish to divest existence of its *rich ambiguity*: that is a dictate of good taste, gentlemen, the taste of reverence for everything that lies beyond your horizon. (*GS*, 335)

The question of *taste* recurs throughout Nietzsche's writing. Christianity is antiquated, old, tasteless. It had become dull, boring, insipid, stale, spoiled, rancid. It smelled and tasted bad; what was heard was laughable, ridiculous; what was seen, the results, were horrifying. He said:

> *A Dangerous Resolve.* — The Christian resolve to find the world ugly and bad has made the world ugly and bad. (*GS*, 185)

Nietzsche refers to Christianity as a fable, a morality tale; as an invention; as an experiment that has failed. He was firm in his belief that men had created the *idea* of God — had created God in their own image, out of their own needs and desires. He was equally convinced that the scientific community was in the process of refuting the idea of the god of Christianity. It is in The *Gay Science* that we find this well-known, often repeated story:

> *The madman.* — Have you not heard of that madman who lit a lantern in the bright morning hours, ran to the market place, and cried incessantly: "I seek God! I seek God! — As many of those who did not believe in God were standing around just then, he provoked much laughter. Has he got lost? Asked one. Did he lose his way like a child? Asked another. Or is he hiding? Is he afraid of us? Has he gone on a voyage? Emigrated? Thus they yelled and laughed.
>
> The madman jumped into their midst and pierced them with his eyes. "Whither is God?" he cried. "I will tell you. *We have killed him* — you and I. All of us are his murderers. But how did we do this? How could we drink up the sea? Who gave us the sponge to wipe away the entire horizon? What were we doing when we unchained this earth from its sun? Whither is it moving now? Whither are we moving? Away from all suns? Are we not plunging continually? Backward, sideward, forward, in all directions? Is there still any up or down? Are we not straying as through an infinite nothing? Do we not feel the breath of empty space? Has it not become colder? Is not night continually closing in on us? Do we not need to light lanterns in the morning? Do we hear nothing as yet of the noise of the gravediggers who are burying God? Do we smell nothing as yet of the divine decomposition? Gods, too,

decompose. God is dead. God remains dead. And we have killed him.

"How shall we comfort ourselves, the murderers of all murderers? What was holiest and mightiest of all that the world has yet owned has bled to death under our knives: who will wipe this blood off us? What water is there for us to clean ourselves? What festivals of atonement, what sacred games shall we have to invent? Is not the greatness of this deed too great for us? Must we ourselves not become gods simply to appear worthy of it? There has never been a greater deed: and whoever is born after us — for the sake of this deed he will belong to a higher history than all history hitherto."

Here the madman fell silent and looked again at his listeners; and they, too, were silent and stared at him in astonishment. At last he threw his lantern on the ground, and it broke into pieces and went out. "I have come too early," he said then; "my time is not yet. This tremendous event is still on its way, still wandering; it has not yet reached the ears of man. Lightning and thunder require time; the light of the stars requires time; deeds, though done, still require time to be seen and heard. This deed is still more distant from them than the most distant stars — *and yet they have done it themselves.*"

It has been related further that on the same day the madman forced his way into several churches and there struck up his *requiem aeternam deo.* Led out and called to account, he is said always to have replied nothing but: "What after all are these churches now if they are not the tombs and sepulchers of God?" (*GS*, 181, 182)

Later in *The Gay Science* he addresses this problem once again when he wrote:

The meaning of our cheerfulness. — The greatest recent event — that "God is dead," that the belief in the Christian god has become unbelievable — is already beginning to cast its first shadows over Europe. For the few at least, whose eyes — the *suspicion* in whose eyes is strong and subtle enough for this spectacle, some sun seems to have set and some ancient and profound trust has been turned into doubt; to them our old world must appear daily more like evening, more mistrustful, stranger, "older." But in the main one may say: The event itself is far too great, too distant, too remote from the multitude's capacity for comprehension even for the tidings of it to be thought of as having *arrived* as yet. Much less may one suppose that many people know as yet *what* this event really means — and how much must collapse now that this faith has been undermined because it was built upon this faith, propped up by it, grown into it; for example, the whole of European morality. This long plenitude and sequence of breakdown, destruction, ruin, and cataclysm that is now impending —

who could guess enough of it today to be compelled to play the teacher and advance proclaimer of the monstrous logic of terror, the prophet of a gloom and an eclipse of the sun whose like has probably never yet occurred on earth? (GS, 279)

This impending breakdown of Christianity, and especially of the morality central to the religion, which was under way, was being met with varying responses. Nietzsche's response was that the demolition must be completed in order for there to be a new beginning, a new understanding of the world, of nature, of life, a "revaluation of all values." One could not build on the remains of the old. He wrote this:

We Europeans confront a world of tremendous ruins. A few things are still towering, much looks decayed and uncanny, while most things already lie on the ground. It is all very picturesque — where has one ever seen such beautiful ruins? — and overgrown by large and small weeds. The church is this city of destruction. We see the religious community of Christianity shaken to its lowest foundations; the faith in God has collapsed; the faith in the Christian-ascetic ideal is still fighting its final battle. An edifice like Christianity that had been built so carefully over such a long period — it was the last construction of the Romans! — naturally could not be destroyed all at once. All kinds of earthquakes had to shake it, all kinds of spirits that bore, dig, gnaw and moisten have had to help. (GS, 310)

Chapter 6. Christianity and Power

For Nietzsche, science was important; art was important; history was important; philosophy was important; religion was important. Also, obviously power, value or values, sexuality, and rank were important. For him to attempt a critique of Christianity apparently meant to engage the religion from all of these perspectives. Having settled on the notion that Christianity was in the throes of a slow, painful, and terminal illness, a slow and torturous downward spiral, it made sense to consider its origin, perhaps also a slow, painful, and difficult birth. It also appeared to have had a robust, carefully guarded and reinforced existence. For something like two centuries Christianity had been not only the dominant narrative in the West, it had been the only narrative, "the greatest story ever told." The narrative had a beginning and an end, coming into existence and going out of existence.

Important among the questions (much like Bachofen) were — what might be understood regarding religious beliefs and practices before the creation of Christianity; and, what were the motive, or motives, and the intention of the founding fathers of this monotheistic, patriarchal religion, the religion which had long been the dominant power or force and foundation of culture, its primary structuring principle.

To the consternation of many of his readers, Nietzsche frequently stresses that he is "an immoralist." And it was morality, the moral values, with which Christianity had secured its dominance, that was at the center of the target of his critique. And, in his thinking, there was no moral order in the universe. Moral values always referred to persons, to the power or powers of an individual. He established early his position regarding *values.* Values do not exist in things or persons. Human beings *create* values, and thereby create a human world. And we constantly change values — devaluing, revaluing — a continuing process. There is the feeling of power in creating values. To change the world, which Nietzsche believed was in desperate need of change, what was required was a radical, revolutionary, reversal of Christian values.

Two short passages in *Beyond Good and Evil* seem to indicate the direction of his thinking. First this:

> Willing seems to me to be, above all, something *complicated*, something that is a unity in word only. The popular judgment lies just in this word "only," and it has become master of the forever incautious philosophers. Let us be more cautious, then; let us be "unphilosophical"; . . . In all willing, then, there is a commanding and obeying. . . . This is why a philosopher should consider himself justified in including willing within the general sphere of morality — morality understood as the doctrine of rank-relations that produce the phenomenon we call "life." — (*BGE*, 19, 21, 22)

These last fourteen words are Nietzsche's first, and major, interpretation of what *morality* means. They lay the groundwork for his critique. The second passage reads:

> What is astonishing about the religiosity of the ancient Greeks is the lavish abundance of gratitude that radiates from it. Only a very distinguished type of human being stands in *that* relation to nature and to life. Later, when the rabble came to rule in Greece, *fear* choked out religion and prepared the way for Christianity. (*BGE*, 58)

Nietzsche makes clear *who* he thinks have been the primary "value-creators." Following the ancient Greeks and their nature religions, the classical Greeks, the *philosophers*, joined later by *theologians* — the founders of Greek philosophy and Christian theology — were the determiners of who has value, power, and rank and who does not have value, power, and rank.

In the opening pages of *Beyond Good and Evil*, Nietzsche is unsparing in his interpretation of philosophers, most of whom he viewed as dogmatists. A look at his words is necessary:

> What tempts us to look at all philosophers half suspiciously and half mockingly is not so much that we recognize again and again how innocent they are, how often and how easily they make mistakes and lose their way, in short their childishness and childlikeness — but rather that they are not sufficiently candid, though they make a great virtuous noisy to-do as soon as the problem of truthfulness is even remotely touched upon. Every one of them pretends that he has discovered and reached his opinions through the self-development of cold, pure, divinely untroubled dialectic (in distinction to the mystics of every rank who, more honest and fatuous, talk about "inspiration"), whereas, at bottom, a pre-conceived dogma, a notion, an "institution," or mostly a heart's desire, made abstract and refined, is defended by them with arguments sought after the fact. . . .

> Gradually I have come to realize what every great philosophy up to now has been: the personal confession of its originator, a type of involuntary and unaware memoirs; also that the moral (or amoral) intention of each philosophy constitute the protoplasm from which each entire plant has grown. Indeed, one will do well (and wisely), if one wishes to explain to himself how on earth the more remote metaphysical assertions of a philosopher ever arose, to ask each time: What sort of morality is this (is *he*) aiming at? Thus I do not believe that a "desire for comprehension" is the father of philosophy, but rather that a quite different desire has here as elsewhere used comprehension (together with miscomprehension) as tools to serve it own ends . . . there is nothing impersonal whatever in the philosopher. And particularly his morality testifies decidedly and decisively as to *who he is* — that is, what order of rank the innermost desires of his nature occupy. (*BGE*, 4, 5, 6, 7)

In his Preface to *Beyond Good and Evil*, this:

> Dogmatic philosophy has been such a grotesque — witness the Vedanta doctrine in Asia and Platonism in Europe. Let us not be ungrateful to it, although it must surely be confessed that the worst, the most tiresome, and the most dangerous of all errors hitherto has been a dogmatist error: namely Plato's invention of Pure Spirit and of the Good in Itself. But now that it has been surmounted, now that Europe, rid of this nightmare, can again draw breath freely and at least enjoy a healthier sleep, now *we whose task it is to stay awake*, we are the heirs of all the power gathered by the fight against this error. To be sure, it meant turning the truth upside down, denying *perspectivity* (the basic condition of life), to speak of Spirit and of the Good as Plato had spoken of them. . . . But the fight against Plato, or — to speak plainer and for "the

people" — the fight against millenniums of Christian-ecclesiastical pressure (for Christianity is Platonism for "the people"), this fight created in Europe magnificent tension of spirit, such as had not existed anywhere before. (*BGE*, xii)

Clearly, Nietzsche's interests in history were to focus on the historical roots and origin, as well as the development, of Christianity. And this took him back to classical Greek philosophy, in particular to Plato. What possible relationship might be detected between the major philosophical doctrines of Platonism and the later inventions of the religious doctrines of Christianity? What possible similarities, or possible differences, might be revealed and of what significance? What contributions might philosophy have offered to religion?

Those historical pursuits drew Nietzsche's attention (reminiscent of Bachofen) back to pre-Classical, ancient religious attitudes, beliefs, and practices as one might understand them through a study of myths and symbols. Uncover similarities? Discern differences? It appears that Nietzsche became increasingly alerted to the possible historical dynamics between philosophy, or philosophers, and theology, or theologians. And tantalizing may have been the fact that fate placed Plato after the centuries of earlier ancient religions and before the arrival of later religions, again especially the Christian religion. Dogmatic philosophy evolving into dogmatic theology — "Platonism for the people."

Briefly, Plato was recognized especially for his invention of the human "soul," in distinction to the human body. And, corresponding to the soul, was his "theory of ideas, or forms," a separate world of eternally unchanging exemplars. The Platonic "soul," more real than the body, of higher rank, of higher value. A similar proclamation regarding the world of ideas — the "real" world, of higher rank and value than the world of mere appearances. With the power of these ideas at hand, Plato was able to argue further for a ranking order which placed "philosopher-kings" at the top of a social hierarchy, of highest power and value.

Remember again, Nietzsche denied that values, and any ranking of values, was something which belonged to our world. We create values, we create any ranking of values. We change values and orders of values. He also appears to have rejected any ranking system which assigns higher value on the basis of membership in groups, classes, types or people. Strictly applied, any designation of value and rank appropriately belonged to the individual person, although he later revised this position.

Christianity borrowed, revived, reinvented, recycled the "soul" and "another world." The founders of Christianity invented their own ideal "true" world, with its own repertoire of freshly conceived ideas — a soul which survives the body after death, an "after-life," heaven, hell, sin, repentance, salvation, sacrifice, and more. In Nietzsche's view, Christianity negated and devalued nature, the natural world, life, the body, sexuality, the senses, the instincts, the passions, procreation, the female. Highest value, power, and rank were assigned to those Nietzsche believed were, in his terms, most "anti-life" — to priests, saints, ascetics. Christianity was a revolt against life, a condemnation of life and of ancient religions and their affirmation and celebration of life.

Hear from Nietzsche. In the Foreword to *Ecce Homo*:

> Reality has been deprived of its value, its meaning, its veracity to the same degree as an ideal world has been *fabricated*. . . . The "real world" and the "apparent world" — in plain terms: the *fabricated* world and reality. . . . The *lie* of the ideal has hitherto been the curse on reality, through it mankind itself has become mendacious and false down to its deepest instincts — to the point of worshipping the *inverse* values to those which alone could guarantee it prosperity, future, the exalted *right* to a future. (*EH*, 34)

In the final chapter of *Ecce Homo*, this:

That contempt has been taught for the primary instincts of life: that a "soul," a "spirit" has been *lyingly invented* in order to destroy the body; that one teaches that there is something unclean in the precondition of life, sexuality; . . . (*EH*, 132)

Near the end of *Twilight of the Idols*, Nietzsche expands further:

> I was the first to take seriously, for the understanding of the older, the still rich even overflowing Hellenic instinct, that wonderful phenomenon which bears the name of Dionysus: it is explicable only in terms of an *excess* of force. . . . For it is only in the Dionysian mysteries, in the psychology of the Dionysian state, that the *basic fact* of the Hellenic instinct finds expression — its "will to life." What was it that the Hellene guaranteed himself by means of these mysteries? *Eternal* life, the eternal return of life; the future promised and hallowed in the past; the triumphant Yes to life beyond all death and change; *true* life as the over-all continuation of life through procreation, through the mysteries of sexuality. For the Greeks the *sexual* symbol was therefore the

venerable symbol par excellence, the real profundity in the whole of ancient piety. Every single element in the act of procreation, of pregnancy, and of birth aroused the highest and most solemn feelings. In the doctrine of the mysteries, *pain* is pronounced holy: the pangs of the woman giving birth hallow all pain; all becoming and growing — all that guarantees a future — involves pain. That there may be the eternal joy of creating, that the will to life may eternally affirm itself, the agony of the woman giving birth *must* also be there eternally.

All this is meant by the word Dionysus: I know of no higher symbolism than this Greek symbolism of the Dionysian festivals. Here the most profound instinct of life, that directed toward the future of life, the eternity of life, is experienced religiously — and the way to life, procreation, as the *holy* way. It was Christianity, with its *resentiment* against life at the bottom of its heart, which first made something unclean of sexuality: it threw *filth* on the origin, on the presupposition of our life. (PN, 560, 561, 562)

Chapter 7. Christianity and Psychology

To remind again of the broad sweep of Nietzsche's interests — art, history, science, philosophy, religion, power, values, sexuality, rank, perspective, interpretation, language or words. His deeper focus and concern were not on these topics, but on those *who* created art, wrote history, engaged in science or philosophy; *who* invented religion and were engaged in religious practices; *who* exercised power, created values and ranking orders; *whose* perspectives and interpretations had prevailed for centuries. His "deep thinking" led him to eventually believe that understanding these cultural creations required the talents of the psychologist — of a philosophical psychologist, a physiological psychologist. In *Beyond Good and Evil* he said this:

> All psychology hitherto has become stuck in moral prejudices and fears: none has ventured into the depths. To consider psychology as the morphology and evolutionary doctrine of the will to power — as I consider it — this no one has touched upon even in thought (insofar as it is allowable to recognize in what has been written the symptoms of what has been kept dark). . . . A proper physio-psychology must battle with unconscious resistances in the heart of the investigator; his "heart" sides against it. . . . But even this hypothesis is by no means the most painful or the strangest in this enormous, almost totally unknown domain of dangerous insights. Indeed, there are a hundred good reasons for staying away from it if one — can! On the other hand, if our ship has once taken us there — very well, let us go ahead, grit our

teeth, open our eyes, grip the rudder and — ride out morality! Perhaps we will crush and destroy our own remaining morality, but what do *we* matter! Never yet has a *deeper* world of insight been opened to bold travelers and adventurers. And the psychologist who can make this sort of "sacrifice" (it is not the *sacrifizio dell' intelletto* — on the contrary!) will at least be in a position to demand that psychology be acknowledged once more as the mistress of the sciences, for whose service and preparation the other sciences exist. For psychology is now again the road to the basic problems. (*BGE*, 26, 27)

There is little doubt that for Nietzsche the "basic problems" which were crystallizing and the "great tasks" which he was setting for himself were increasingly being formed within the context of his attempted critique of Christianity. He was setting out to challenge, penetrate, and expose what he believed was a web of deceit and lies. He knew that he was taking on the follies and untruths of the powerful that had predominated for centuries. As with Bachofen, Nietzsche had come to believe that religion, i.e. Christianity, had been the primary power, the foundation of Western culture for two millennia. His aim was to discredit and demolish the belief system and institutions, not with "gunpowder" but with words, against a formidable, tyrannical, and dangerous adversary. And the "new psychology," (himself as the "new psychologist") would be his guide. New and dangerous questions were demanded.

Nietzsche's philosophy of power was also a psychology of power. And who better able to challenge what he saw as the sustained force of Christianity than himself, who had developed, or was developing, probably the most comprehensive theory of power in human history. So, a reconsideration of the subject is needed. Recall, his cosmological interpretation was that "this world is a monster of energy" — power which may astound, terrify, or inspire awe. This is how he perceived, how he interpreted this *natural* world. And, he considered this a scientific, physical theory rather than a typically philosophical metaphysical theory. Remember these words:

[D]o you want a *name* for this *world*? A *solution* for all your riddles? A *light* for you too, you best concealed, strongest, least dismayed, most midnight men? — *This world is the will to power — and nothing beside!* And you yourself are also this will to power — and nothing beside! (*N*, 136)

Nietzsche's theory was meant to apply, of course, to both the animate and the inanimate. And, of course, his concern was with the animate, living things, plants and animals, to all living things — to *life*. In living things, especially in humans, this will to power might be considered as an impulse or inner drive. That is, as a *motive*, literally, "that which moves a person to action, to set or keep in motion" — a force so communicated as to produce motion, physiological activity. The theory was intended to explain, or interpret, human nature and human behavior, *every* kind of human behavior, every human action. Also, *all* inner experience — emotions, desires, aversions, instincts, feelings, wishes, passions, ideas, beliefs, and more — *everything* that is part of life. But this theory, which he considered as being a scientific theory, was intended as an experimental idea, to be reflected upon, tested — never accepted as dogma or doctrine.

The will to power, the drive to power as the basic drive in humans, was continuously expressing, exercising, discharging — displaying itself, or manifesting itself in multiple senses, given multiple meanings. The many senses, or meanings, attached to the idea of power perhaps support the idea of the ubiquity and the ambiguity of power. Consider power as — energy, ability, capability, capacity, strength, might, force, influence, inspire, persuade, authority, arouse, dominate, control, command.

There is little doubt that Nietzsche's thinking about power reflected the ancient idea of power experienced and understood as the energy and ability to *create* — creativity, or generative power. The power to create life, values, names, ideas, words, images, oneself, and more. To create more power, as well as the counterparts — intimidation, obedience, weakness, punishment, destruction. The basic expression of power was the *power to create life*, the origin of life, the physiology of the human body, sexuality.

Two important relationships referred to earlier need to be reaffirmed. First, in elaborating his theory of will to power, he holds the idea that *power* is the standard of all *values* — the value of persons, of human actions, or things. Power, or powers, is in the world, in all of nature. However, regarding values, recall again what he says:

Whatever has value in our world does not have value in itself, according to its nature — nature is always value-less, but has been given value at some time as a present — and it was *we* who gave and bestowed it. Only we have created the world *that concerns man!* — But precisely this knowledge we lack, and when we occasionally catch it for a fleeting moment we always forget it again immediately; we fail to recognize our best power and underestimate ourselves, the contemplatives, just a little. We are *neither as proud nor as happy* as we might be. (*GS*, 242)

Power and *value* are inextricably related in the human world. The second fundamental relationship following from these two is the relation between power and rank. Not only are values created by human persons, *we* also create orders of rank among values. Rank is not "in the world." Power is the determiner of rank. Importantly, values and rank — the ordering of values — are constantly in flux, never stable, constantly changing or being changed. Although never absolute, objective, permanent, eternal, or certain, values and an order, or rank, of values form the foundation, the basic structuring principle of any human culture. They are the driving force of history. One major expression of the will to power is the drive to establish a system of rank, of command and control, and to give arguments to justify such an order. Nietzsche was well aware of the hierarchical orders, particularly in both the Catholic Church and the Prussian state. So, in extending his philosophy of the will to power, we have the inextricable connections among *power, value,* and *rank* — actually the heart of his theory of power. Perhaps we could call this the "p/v/r factor." It was the basis for his critique of Christianity — which became his primary project, his "great task."

Nietzsche could have chosen to leave the mounting criticism of Christianity to the scientific rationalists and chosen to merely abandon his religion in becoming an atheist. However, all of his thinking appears to have been driving him in a very different and much deeper direction. And much more dangerous.

From among the thousands of words that Nietzsche used in speaking about Christianity, it seems appropriate to recount several of the ways in which he perceived, interpreted, and portrayed his subject. Many of his characterizations seem intended to shock his readers.

Christianity was a fable, a fantasy version of the world, a short tale intending to teach a moral. It was an invention, a failed or failing experiment. It was an error, a web of deceit, a "Holy Lie." sanctified, constantly revised, updated, reaffirmed, enforced — (reminiscent of Plato's "Noble Lie.") It was, or had become, tasteless, dull, boring, insipid, antiquated, therefore of little or no value. It was a revolt against life, a condemnation of life. It was a revolt against human intelligence. It was increasingly being perceived as a view of the world disconnected from the real world. It was, in Nietzsche's thinking, the primary source of — and therefore responsible for — the deteriorating, decadent, decomposing, disintegrating condition of European or Western culture — tyrannical and dangerous.

Nietzsche's consuming task had become to access, penetrate, challenge, analyze, interpret, expose, subvert, not the rationality of Christianity but rather the *power of Christianity* — the power structure, power politics, power dynamics. He sought to probe the origins, especially the originators or inventors; the sources, the abuses, the corruptions, the dangers, the devastating consequences of the decadence, and the magnitude of that power. And, most of all, what was at the heart or core of that power.

Nietzsche's credentials for his task were extraordinary. At the age of twenty he went to Bonn University as a student of theology and classical philology. He subsequently abandoned theology, began to develop his interests in philosophy, and became a classical philologist. He is considered as having been a philosopher. It is difficult, if not impossible, however, not to recognize how inextricably his philosophy is interwoven with his philology. And later with his psychology. His attraction to, his love of, learning, literature, understanding, wisdom, speech, words, was all-consuming.

As for his philosophy, his philology, and his psychology, Nietzsche saw himself as ushering in a new period of momentous change. Regarding philosophy and philosophers, many, if not most, of whom he viewed as dogmatists, he wrote:

> We must wait for a new species of philosopher to arrive, who will have some other, opposite tastes and inclinations than the previous ones. Philosophers of the Perilous Perhaps, in every sense! And seriously, I can see such new philosophers coming up over the horizon. . . . I risk baptizing them with a name that is not devoid of peril. As I read them (as they allow themselves to be read — for it is characteristic of their type that they wish to remain rid-

dles in some sense), these philosophers of the future have a right (perhaps also a wrong!) to be called: *Experimenters.* This name itself is only an experiment, and, if you will, a temptation. . . . After all this need I say especially that they shall be free, *very* free thinkers, these philosophers of the future? (*BGE*, 3, 48, 49)

Nietzsche, himself, served as the prototype for this new emerging philosopher — this "Philosopher of the Perilous Perhaps."

Although he never referred to himself as a "new philologist," there is reason enough to give him that name. There seems to be reason enough also to suggest the strong possibility that his years of association, or friendship, with Bachofen opened up a whole new and exciting world to supplement his interests in classical, especially Greek philology. Bachofen was a philologist more focused on Roman philology. Both were captives of philology — literally, the love of learning, literature, words, speech, spoken or written. It was a field of study that sheds light on cultural history. Bachofen's was a major scholarly voice arguing for a reconsideration, reinterpretation, and revaluation of myths and symbols. He was a mythologist and symbologist. As both, he perceived mythology, not as spurious or false, but as a branch of knowledge — significant, legitimate, and necessary. A myth is a "traditional story of ostensibly historical events that serves to unfold part of the world view of a people, or explain a practice, belief, or natural phenomenon — a pattern of beliefs expressing, often symbolically, the characteristics or prevalent attitudes in a group or culture." A symbol is "an act, sound, or object having cultural significance and the capacity to excite or objectify a response," e.g., symbolic dance.

Mythological speech, having preceded classical philosophical, or Christian theological speech, was to be viewed and heard as equally authentic. Bachofen interpreted these myths as being religious in nature, a kind of "natural religion." This interpretation seems to reflect a traditional view of religion as "response of awe regarding the mysterious *powers of nature*; any set of beliefs concerning the cause, nature, purpose of the universe; usually involving devotion, ritual observances; often containing moral codes governing conduct of human affairs, beliefs, devotion; often personified in gods and goddesses."

Bachofen, himself, could also be called a "new philologist." With a close reading of Nietzsche's writings, one may claim the following.

He did agree with Bachofen's interpretation as to the authenticity, the status, and the necessity of carefully studying myths and symbols in enriching our knowledge of the past. He agreed with Bachofen's interpretation that the changes from ancient cultures to the present could be fruitfully considered as some type of evolutionary process. He agreed that religion had been, and continued to be, the primary force in structuring culture, the basis of culture. He agreed in the continuity between biological life and cultural life — the centrality of sexuality, male and female.

Nietzsche was not in agreement, however, with either the specific language used, or the specific reading of the process of change by Bachofen. In reading Nietzsche, one does not find stress on the terms matriarchy or patriarchy, maternal or paternal. His language reflects his philosophical interests — for the most part. Power, values, rank, words, perspective, experience, ideas, morality — these were the sorts of words in Nietzsche's lexicon.

As for his interpretation of the process of change, Bachofen used an evolutionary, linear model, moving in one direction, from lower to higher forms. Nietzsche's preference decidedly favored a cyclic model (perhaps somewhat complicated by the widespread popularity and theoretical application of Hegel's notion of a dialectical interpretation of history). More about this later.

CHAPTER 8. CHRISTIANITY AND MORALITY

A "new philosopher," a "new philologist," and as we have heard, a "new psychologist." And remember, he referred to this new psychology, or psychologist, as "physio-psychology," which "must battle with unconscious resistance in the heart of the investigator. . . ." Physiological psychology, sometimes called psychophysiology, is a branch of psychology that deals with the effects of normal and pathological physiological processes on mental life. Also, as we noted earlier, Nietzsche realized the probability that this new type of psychological investigation might reveal "an almost totally unknown domain of dangerous insights." And he added, "Perhaps we will crush and destroy our own remaining morality, but what do *we* matter! Never yet has a *deeper* world of insight been opened to bold travelers and adventurers." A torturous and dangerous adventure for a very deep thinker — himself.

Nietzsche's *great task* was to expose and subvert the power of Christianity. And he well understood that this power resided in words, in speech, oral and written. And Nietzsche's power was in words, in speech — almost entirely in written words, for hardly anyone in his own time was able to "hear" him. His power, i.e., energy and abilities, as the new philosopher, new philologist, and new psychologist, was more than adequate for his task. He hardly needed to remind himself that "In the beginning was the Word, and the Word was with God, and the word was God."

Nietzsche was acutely conscious of the dangers involved with, and surrounding, his adventure. He had spoken of the "uncanny dangerousness" of Christianity itself. He had spoken of the dangerous character of his own thinking and writing. And he was keenly aware of the necessity of prudence in concealing and disguising the true nature of his mission — his "mask" and other related devices. He was well acquainted with the history of the responses of the church fathers to perceived acts of heresy or apostasy. Also, some of his immediate predecessors, including Bachofen, Marx, and Darwin were already beginning to be seen as a threat to Christian orthodoxy. It was important and timely for him to take elaborate precautions to be "misunderstood."

Now is the time to venture bringing together these scattered tangled strands of Nietzsche's thinking into his possible coherent critique of Christianity. Christianity had been brought into existence for the purpose of changing the world — by changing the values, primarily moral values, morality — by establishing a new order of power. Moral values, or morality, is at the heart of Nietzsche's critique and we will return to this a little later. Now, however, just this brief reminder from *Beyond Good and Evil*:

> It is obvious that the moral value-characteristics are at first applies to *people* and only later, in a transferred sense, to *acts*. (*BGE*, 203)

Consistent with Nietzsche's interpretation of the will to power, that *all* human behavior may be understood as a drive, or impulse, toward power, the basic original motive, the motive of the founders of religions — in his case, of Christianity — was power. The purpose, or end, was to acquire, maintain, and increase power — their own. And, of course, it was the power of words — spoken, written, or sung, supplemented with symbolic speech — physical violence — that would accomplish victory.

The "priestly types" had developed a compelling repertoire — a supply of skills, devices, capabilities with which to accomplish this purpose. It had been planned and carried out with care and precision. It was Nietzsche's task to dismantle, or disentangle, the numerous means of expressing, or exercising, power which had been compiled and honed during many centuries.

At the top of the list was the ability, the power, to create *deception*, *lies* — to deceive, to develop what he calls "a web of deceit." Recall, Nietzsche had referred to Christianity as a fable, "a story invented to entertain or deceive, usually teaching a moral lesson and without basis in reality." He also used the term fabrication — "carefully invented, created, made up, for the purpose of deceiving." And deceiving meant "imposing a false idea or belief that causes ignorance, bewilderment, or helplessness" — weakness, inability to act. The "web of deceit" was the ability to delude, "to deceive so thoroughly as to obscure the truth."

The notion of *reversal* was fundamental to Nietzsche's thought, so it was not surprising that he applied the idea in his thinking about Christianity. Ancient nature religions had affirmed the "truth" of nature, of life, the body, sexuality. These were celebrations, glorifying the awesome powers of nature, life, body, the creative power of the female, the maternal. The response of Christianity was reactive, negation, denial, in opposition to, hostile to, these earlier forms of worship, celebrating instead the power of the male, the paternal. Christianity had endeavored to deprive these earlier expressions of their continuing existence, or value. Old religions, if resisting destruction, were assimilated or absorbed into the new form. Mythical history was devalued, discredited, as mere fiction, deserving no serious consideration. In Nietzsche's view, Christianity was anti-nature, anti-life, anti-body, anti-sexuality, anti-female. And it had set out to devalue all of these — a "transvaluation of values." It had turned truth upside down. Recall also from *Beyond Good and Evil*:

> What is astonishing about the religiosity of the ancient Greeks is the lavish abundance of gratitude that radiates from it. Only a very distinguished type of human being stands in *that* relation to nature and to life. Later, when the rabble came to rule in Greece, *fear* choked out religion and prepared the way for Christianity. (*BGE*, 58)

From its earliest beginnings, Christianity had preached and promoted intimidation, inducing fear or a sense of inferiority, where courage is lost. It had preached dependence, and especially obedience. This indoctrination served to invest the founders and "priestly-types" with

increasing authority, control, command. Those in positions of authority encouraged, even demanded, that the Christian message be dissemi-
nated throughout the world, that converts be sought by those already
believers of the faith, thereby increasing the power, or the feeling of
power, of both the leaders and the followers.

The power of Christianity was manifested not only in words, or
speaking, but also in restricting or forbidding critical, or opposing,
voices. Control of who was allowed to speak, where and when speaking was permitted, and what speech was permissible was indispensable to the success of Christianity. The formidable power of *silence* was
exercised, particularly with respect to so-called heretics — those who
were perceived as having dissented from established accepted belief or
established church dogma, and to apostates — those who renounced
the faith.

The magnitude of the power of Christianity, which Nietzsche understood was the power of words, revealed itself not only in its deceptive and destructive qualities, but also in its creative, or inventive, ability. The designers and builders had created and successfully marketed
"new things" — names, images, symbols, rules, laws, values, which they
had cleverly woven together to produce an intricate narrative, that
"web of deceit." These threads included and highlighted — God, world,
soul, devil, sin, heaven, hell, salvation, guilt, redemption, resurrection,
immortality, repentance, confession, sacrifice, conscience, prayer. A
few of these seem to form the nucleus of the destructive power of this
narrative. First, of course, is God.

The image, or representation, of the Christian god is the contrary
of the many gods and goddesses of the ancient religions. In the earlier versions, these multiple deities were usually represented as having "human, all too human" qualities, and especially various, specific,
and *limited* powers. In the Christian version, the single deity, God, is
personified as the embodiment of all power, *unlimited* power, as well
as unlimited knowledge or wisdom, and perfect goodness. From the
human world of human limitations was conceived, imagined, a figure
without limitations. In the ancient religions the dominant deity was
represented almost always as female, the maternal, the great earth goddess — the original trinity of the virgin, the mother, and the crone.

Across many cultures and with her many names, ancient myths testify to the dominance of the female deity in the pre-classical, pre-Hellenic era. The single representation in the Christian version was in direct opposition, the antithesis, the second stage of a dialectical process — the sole god, male, paternal, the heavenly god. The transfer of power from the perception of human limited power to unlimited power was "earth-shaking."

This newly-created, perfect, ideal, male god required a new abode, another world, a new ideal domain in which absolute dominion and power is exercised. Nietzsche spoke frequently about ideals, i.e., ideas existing *only* as mental images. Regarding one of his last books, *Twilight of the Idols*, he makes clear that when he speaks of idols, i.e., false conceptions, false gods, he is speaking about ideals. Here is one late example from his last book, *Ecce Homo*:

> I erect no new idols; let the old idols learn what it means to have legs of clay. *To overthrow idols* (my word for "ideals") — that rather is my business. Reality has been deprived of its value, its meaning, its veracity to the same degree as an ideal world has been *fabricated*. . . . The "real world" and the "apparent world" — in plain terms: the *fabricated* world and reality. . . . The *lie* of the ideal has hitherto been the curse on reality, through it mankind itself has become mendacious and false down to its deepest instincts — to the point of worshipping the *inverse* values to those which alone could guarantee its prosperity, future, the exalted *right* to a future. (*EH*, 34)

Another image at the heart of the Christian narrative was that of the Platonic "soul," some immaterial, spiritual essence, or principle, animating and distinct from the body. Nietzsche was relentless in his condemnation of the value which Christianity had placed on the ideal, the soul, and the disvalue which had been assigned to the body. As he often remarked, Christianity was "anti-body." Nietzsche reminds us that the human body is the primary phenomenon in this world of appearances, the primary object known through the senses, constantly perceived as a process of changing, of developing, in a constant state of "becoming" — from birth to death. The body was not a mental image, or idea. He reminded us also that the ancients had celebrated the body, valued the body; Plato and later philosophers had misunderstood and devalued the body; Christianity had further denigrated and devalued the body; and, during the Renaissance the body had been revalued and revived, especially in the arts. Remember these words:

> That contempt has been taught for the primary instincts of life; that a "soul," a "spirit" has been *lyingly invented* in order to destroy the body; that one teaches that there is something unclean in the precondition of life, sexuality; . . . (*EH*, 132)

One of Nietzsche's most direct and unyielding attacks on this idol is in one of "Zarathustra's Speeches," entitled "On the Despisers of the Body":

> I want to speak to the despisers of the body. I would not have them learn and teach differently, but merely say farewell to their own bodies — and thus become silent.
>
> "Body am I, and soul" — thus speaks the child. And why should one not speak like children?
>
> But the awakened and knowing say: body am I entirely, and nothing else; and soul is only a word for something about the body. . . .
>
> [Y]ou are angry with life and the earth. An unconscious envy speaks out of the squint-eyed glance of your contempt. (*Z*, 34, 35)

And then there is, in the Christian narrative, sin. Nietzsche tells us that Greek antiquity was a world without feelings of sin, "which still seems so very strange to our sensibility." In *The Gay Science*, he responds to his own question as to the origin of sin:

> The Christian presupposes a powerful, overpowering being who enjoys revenge. His power is so great that nobody could possibly harm him, except for his honor. Every sin is a slight to his honor, a *crimen laesae majestatis divinae* — and no more. Contrition, degrada-tion, rolling in the dust — all this is the first and last condition of his grace: in sum the restoration of his divine honor. Whether the sin has done any other harm, whether it has set in motion some profound calamity that will grow and seize one person af-ter another like a disease and strangle them — this honor-craving Oriental in heaven could not care less! Sin is an offense against him, not against humanity. Those who are granted his grace are also granted this carelessness regarding the natural consequenc-es of sin. God and humanity are separated so completely that a sin against humanity is really unthinkable: every deed is to be considered *solely with respect to its supernatural consequences* without regard for its natural consequences; . . . (*GS*, 187, 188)

The invented idea of sin is dependent for its meaning on the invent-ed idea of God. Those who invented the image of the Christian god also invented the image of sin as the violation of God's laws or commands. Nietzsche was, no doubt, aware also that the origin of sin in the Chris-tian tradition was the imputation of this violation to the woman with the biblical name of Eve, called "Mother of All Living." Sin first entered the world through the mother.

Heaven and hell, two additional spaces other than earth, reimagined in the process of creating the Christian narrative. The expanse of space that seems to be over the earth like a dome became the dwelling place of the deity, the eternal place of those rewarded and chosen by God, the place of eternal happiness of the blessed — heaven. The expanse of space that seems to be under the earth, in earlier ancient narratives was imagined as dark, mysterious, and awesome, perhaps fearsome. In the reimagining of Christianity, it became a torture chamber, the eternal place of those eternally punished by God for sins and wickedness. The diabolical image of hell seemed to be the ultimate expression of revenge by a vengeful god — or by those who invented the Christian doctrines.

With the exception of the new imaging of the god of Christianity — from earlier versions of multiple female and male deities with limited powers to a single deity with unlimited powers — probably no other thread of the "grand narrative" was as crucial for the eventual success of Christianity as resurrection and immortality. A god with infinite power, in creating man in his own image, had to bestow on his creation infinite life, immortality.

From earlier views which accepted and affirmed death as part of life, life as finite, the new image was of a benevolent god exercising his power in the ultimate gift of eternal life. Nietzsche's interpretation of the "lavish abundance of gratitude" toward nature and life that radiated from the religiosity of the ancients, and predated Christianity, stands in sharp contrast to the gratitude evoked toward God and for the promise of immortality.

There was another factor regarding the thinking and speaking of the founders and maintainers of Christianity that Nietzsche believed had contributed immeasurably to its victory and long successful regime. Early in his career, remember, he had deliberately adopted his unique *style*, one which he considered necessary in speaking his own very dangerous thoughts. So, he was very cognizant of the significance of style for these Christian speakers. Nietzsche had adopted and developed his style to cover his "truth." Christianity had adopted and developed the style that would serve to cover what Nietzsche believed were their "lies." And this style? It was intentionally the style of power — authoritarian, unconditional, categorical, absolute, certain, dogmatic, dictatorial, infallible. Christianity had developed doctrines concerning faith and morality formally stated and in authoritative proclamations. God was absolute and perfect. The truth of Christianity was absolute. The speaking of priests, and "priestly types," might be described as "sanctimonious pontification" — sanctimonious meaning "hypocritical, or false, giving the appearance of virtue or religious devotion"; pontification meaning "to speak, express one's opinions, in pompous, dogmatic fashion." This speaking was the means to their own power — to make rules, commands for others to live by, to proclaim values. Nietzsche's intention was to challenge not only the message of Christianity, but also the messengers.

For Nietzsche, the "scientific philosopher," the "contrarian," this mode of thinking and speaking had to be rejected. It had deceived many people for too long. Its destructive power was evident. Also, recall that Nietzsche had concluded that most, if not all, great philosophers before him had been dogmatists. And in his interpretation of their philosophizing, he asked this question:

> What sort of morality is this (is *he*) aiming at? Thus I do not believe that a "desire for comprehension" is the father of philosophy, but rather that a quite different desire has here as elsewhere used comprehension (together with miscomprehension) as tools to serve its own ends. . . .
>
> Conversely, there is nothing impersonal whatever in the philosopher. And particularly his morality testifies decidedly and decisively as to *who he is* — that is, what order of rank the innermost desires of his nature occupy. (*BGE*, 6, 7)

And a similar charge could be made against theologians — thus Nietzsche believed. The power being sought, and which had been developed and achieved, by the founders and "priestly types" of Christianity, was the power residing in its moral values, its morality. All else, all other new or revised images, were for the sake of this order of rank. All of the other ideas in the Christian narrative were invented to support, reinforce, guarantee, justify what Nietzsche called "slave-morality" — primarily the idea of the Christian god.

The greatest threat, the "uncanny dangerousness" of Christianity, the heart of the Christian doctrine, was its moral values, its *morality*. And that morality had been spread throughout much of the Western world. It became the principle for structuring the entire Western culture. More of this later.

Of all the vast amount of Nietzsche's speaking about morality, two definite and explicit meanings of the term form the basis of his critical analysis. His earlier definition in *Beyond Good and Evil* reads:

> [M]orality understood as the doctrine of the rank-relations that produce the phenomenon we call "life" — (*BGE*, 22)

Clear and precise. What, if not the ranking of the sexes? And Nietzsche names himself "an immoralist" countless times, even claiming to be the "first immoralist."

The second definition was written in the last chapter of his last book — "Why I Am a Destiny," in *Ecce Homo*. A few excerpts lead up to this definition:

> At bottom my expression *immoralist* involves two denials. I deny first a type of man who has hitherto counted as the highest, the *good*, the *benevolent*, beneficent; I deny secondly a kind of morality which has come to be accepted and to dominate as morality in itself — *decadence* morality, in more palpable terms *Christian* morality. . . .
>
> Have I been understood? — What defines me, what sets me apart from all the rest of mankind, is that I have *unmasked* Christian morality. That is why I needed a word which would embody the sense of a challenge to everyone. Not to have opened its eyes here sooner counts to me as the greatest piece of uncleanliness which humanity has on its conscience, as self-deception becomes instinct, as a fundamental will *not* to observe every event, every cause, every reality. . . . Blindness in the face of Christianity is the *crime par excellence* — the crime *against life*. . . . And that is in fact *my* insight: the teachers, the leaders of mankind, theologians included, have also one and all been *decadents: thence* the revaluation of all values into the inimical to life, *thence* morality. . . . *Definition of* morality: morality — the idiosyncrasy of *decadents* with the hidden intention of *revenging themselves on life* — and successfully. I set store by *this* definition. —
>
> Have I been understood? I have not just now said a word that I could not have said five years ago through the mouth of Zarathustra. — The *unmasking* of Christian morality is an event without equal, a real catastrophe. He who exposes it is a *force majeure*, a destiny — he breaks the history of mankind into two parts. One lives *before* him, one lives *after* him. . . . (*EH*, 128, 131, 132, 133)

Chapter 9. Christianity and Sexuality

Nietzsche believed that one had only to *choose* to open one's eyes to observe that the producers of "life" — natural or cultural — were males and females. All other distinctions — race, ethnicity, class, etc. — were derivative and secondary. Also, it was clearly perceivable that the rank-relations between the sexes had been established from the very beginning of Christian ideology. Also, there was no disputing that it was clear that this relationship was such as to designate the male as superior and dominant, the female as inferior and submissive. In Nietzsche's view, this arrangement was not an incidental element of Christianity. It was, and continued to be, the core, the essential and enduring element, the aim of this religion from its inception. It was the power which had been intended, sought, and achieved, incredibly successfully.

Nietzsche was aware, however, that this way of thinking probably was not entirely original. Recall this from *Beyond Good and Evil*:

> What is astonishing about the religiosity of the ancient Greeks is the lavish abundance of gratitude that radiates from it. Only a very distinguished type of human being stands in *that* relation to nature and to life. Later, when the rabble came to rule in Greece, *fear* choked out religion and prepared the way for Christianity. (*BGE*, 58)

Perhaps the "rabble" to whom he was referring were Socrates, Plato, and Aristotle. Nietzsche had shown his distaste, even scorn, for both Socrates and Plato. But what about Aristotle? His role in preparing the way for Christianity was major. And not only in preparing the way, as we shall see. Nietzsche could hardly have been unfamiliar with Aristotle's writings — one of those "dogmatic" philosophers.

Aristotle was the first major Western theoretician to address directly, and at length, the relative status of the female and the male. Considering the overall magnitude of Aristotle's influence on the development of Western ideas and culture, including especially religious thinking, it seems apparent that at least a brief incursion into this particular analysis should be ventured. Of particular interest for this issue are first, his biological writings, especially "The Generation of Animals," in which he analyzes the respective roles of the male and the female in the reproduction of life. And second, his political writings, *Politics*, in which his concern is the social and political status of the woman. The first major figure to offer a new "scientific biology," extraordinarily detailed, if extravagantly contrived and convoluted, Aristotle maintains that woman is a mutilated and incomplete man — a thesis that has had a long and persistent history. His theory depends on his claim that women have less "soul" than men. What this comes to is that the male contributes the "form," or soul, while the female contributes merely the "matter," or nutrition. That is, the male creates human life, not the female.

Having established, in his view, the authoritative position regarding the obviously deficient natural state of the woman, Aristotle proceeds to argue that she is physically weaker and is less capable of rational thought. All to reassure that the subordinate position of the female is justifiably necessary and rational. A few examples of his writing suggest the range of his more or less "scientific observations" and inferences:

> In all cases, excepting those of the bear and leopard, the female is less spirited than the male; in regard to the two exceptional cases, the superiority in courage rests with the female. With all other animals the female is softer in disposition than the male, is more mischievous, less simple, more impulsive, and more attentive to the nurture of the young; the male, on the other hand, is more spirited than the female, more savage, more simple and less cunning. . . . (IW, 48)

The fact is, the nature of man is the most rounded off and complete, and consequently in man the qualities or capacities above referred to are found in their perfection. Hence woman is more compassionate than man, more easily moved to tears, at the time is more jealous, more querulous, more apt to scold and to strike. She is, furthermore, more prone to despondency and less hopeful than the man, more void of shame or self-respect, more false of speech, more deceptive, and of more retentive memory. She is also more wakeful, more shrinking, more difficult to rouse to action, and requires a smaller quantity of nutriment. (*IW*, 49)

And therefore we must study the man who is in the most perfect state both of body and soul, for in him we shall see the true relation of the two; although in bad or corrupted natures the body will often appear to rule over the soul, because they are in an evil and unnatural condition. . . . (*IW*, 51)

And it is clear that the rule of the soul over the body, and of the mind and the rational element over the passionate is natural and expedient; whereas the equality of the two or the rule of the inferior is always hurtful. (*IW*, 51)

Again, the male is by nature superior, and the female inferior; and the one rules and the other is ruled; this principle, of necessity, extends to all mankind. (*IW*, 51)

The relation of the male to the female is of this kind, but there the inequality is permanent. . . . (*IW*, 52, 53)

[T]he courage and justice of a man and of a woman, are not, as Socrates maintained, the same; the courage of a man is shown in commanding, of a woman in obeying. (*IW*, 54)

All classes must be deemed to have their special attributes; as the poet says of women, "Silence is a woman's glory," but this is not equally the glory of the man. . . . (*IW*, 54)

It might be relatively persuasive to claim that more than any other figure, Aristotle was the "father" of Western intellectual and cultural history — that is, considering the last two and a half millennia. He announced the emergence of the patriarchal mode of analysis, interpretation, and speaking. And he did this brilliantly. What followed were, in a sense, footnotes, annotations, elaborations. His thinking was acclaimed, celebrated, embraced, rejected, denied, rebutted, but rarely ignored. A notable ranking member of Aristotle's genealogy was the thirteenth-century theologian, Thomas Aquinas. Aristotle was the darling of Aquinas.

By the thirteenth century the thinking about woman had been well established in the medieval church by Paul and Augustine. However, the real heavyweight in Christian theology was Aquinas, with his remarkable synthesis between the Judeo-Christian and Greek traditions, especially Aristotle. Aquinas agreed with Aristotle's perspective that woman is a defective male, lacking in vital force, a "misbegotten," "deformed," "contemptible," creature. From a Christian perspective, God created woman in the divine order, and her deformity is therefore natural. Aristotle's "scientific biology" in no way contradicted Aquinas' "biblical biology." The details of Aquinas' interpretation of the validity and morality of woman's natural inferiority and social subordination are as contrived and convoluted as those of his esteemed and beloved philosopher. The *Summa Theologica* of Aquinas was destined to provide the Roman Catholic Church with its official theological and philosophical dogma for centuries to come. And that included its treatment of women, one major aspect of which was the silencing of the female voice.

His father having been a pastor, his having first studied theology as his life's work, and his having become what he called a "Christian philologist," seem to assure that Nietzsche knew Aquinas well — and also, of course, Aristotle. From Nietzsche's perspective, this ranking in value and ability, i.e., power, of the sexes was not an incidental, accidental aspect of Christianity. It was the centerpiece, the intended purpose, the power imbalance which had carefully been created. It was what Nietzsche meant by its morality, that which he intended to expose, and did.

Nietzsche, we know, was also a biologist, but of a different persuasion, from a different "scientific" perspective. His concern was with human living organisms and their vital processes. Rejecting the existence of any separate soul, humans — male or female — are entirely bodies, created by means of the natural sexual functions of procreation and birth. With the developing new sciences, the human body was becoming the subject of knowledge of the anatomy, the physiology, and the medical treatment of bodies. The knowledge sought by Nietzsche was not of the analysis or examination of the body as a physical phenomenon, but rather the *experience* and *consciousness* one has of one's own body, as well as of others with either similar or different bodies. His physiological psychology was intended to study the phenomenon of the multifarious and complicated ways one might have of responding to, or experiencing, one's body. It was the science of psychology that was his concern. And it was primarily the sexual physiology — experience, not analysis.

CHAPTER 10. CHRISTIANITY AND RESENTMENT

From his perspective of the physiological psychologist, Nietzsche was directing his attention beyond, or behind, or beneath the morality of Christianity to questions regarding the psychology of those responsible for inventing and reinventing their doctrine of moral values. His sleuthing took him much further into dangerous territory — of the psyche. Dangerous for himself and for others, and — perhaps the most torturous part of his investigations — requiring the ultimate amount of integrity and honesty. Honesty, he told us, is the youngest of the virtues, and perhaps the most difficult to acquire.

His questions centered on who were the sources, the creators of the Christian narrative; what did they hope, or expect, to gain; what was their motive, or motives; what complex psychological phenomena might be in play? And after relentless probing, his diagnosis was stark, harsh, blunt, shocking, even unbelievable. And not surprisingly, his philological and philosophical learning helped in his becoming alert to the signs and symptoms, and the dangers involved.

Aristotle was familiar with Hesiod, and Nietzsche was familiar with both. Hesiod, Greek epic poet, who is believed to have lived approximately nine hundred years before Christ, has been described as follows:

Hesiod is the poet of the roadside grass and the many-colored earth, and of men who live by the soil. Echoes of ancient peasant wisdom, and of the mysteries of the earth, linger in his pages. (*H*, cover)

Hesiod produced three major works: the *Theogony*, the *Catalog of Women* or *Eoiai*, and *The Works and Days*. The same interpreter says, "He is, in a way, the first Greek theologian, and so in a vaguer way, the first philosopher." In *The Works and Days*, Hesiod interprets the history of man's life as having occurred in five descending ages, or generations — the golden age, the silver age, the bronze age, the heroic age, and the iron age — the fifth and present age. Giving an account of the strife and violence which characterizes this age he writes:

> And I wish that I were not any part
>   of the fifth generation
> of men, but had died before it came,
>   or been born afterward...
> The spirit of Envy, with grim face
>   and screaming voice, who delights
> In evil, will be the constant companion
>   of wretched humanity,
> And at last Nemesis and Aidos, Decency and Respect,
>   shrouding
> their bright forms in pale mantles, shall go
>   from the wide-wayed
> earth back on their way to Olympos,
>   forsaking the whole race
> of mortal men, and all that will be left by them
>   to mankind
> will be wretched pain. And there shall be no defense
>   against evil. (*H*, 41, 43)

It is likely that Hesiod was one of the earliest writers to perceive the enormous significance and power of this phenomenon of *envy*. Envy, he was cautioning, and which he described in distressing words, was definitive of the present age — meaning a period of time dominated by a prominent feature.

In his *Rhetoric*, Aristotle gives perhaps one of the most concise, systematic interpretations of envy, one to influence many future considerations of the phenomenon. That Aristotle's discussion influenced Nietzsche's thinking is hardly deniable and gives reason to repeating some of his words:

To take Envy next: we can see on what grounds, against what persons, and in what states of mind we feel it. Envy is pain at the sight of such good fortune as consists of the good things already mentioned; we feel it towards our equals; not with the idea of getting something for ourselves, but because the other people have it. We shall feel it if we have, or think we have, equals; and by "equals" I mean equals in birth, relationship, age, disposition, distinction, or wealth. We feel envy also if we fall but a little short of having everything; which is why people in high place and prosperity feel it — they think every one else is taking what belongs to themselves. Also if we are exceptionally distinguished for some particular thing, and especially if that thing is wisdom or good fortune. . . . We also envy those whose possession of or success in a thing is a reproach to us; these are our neighbors and equals; . . . Emulation makes us take steps to secure the good things in question, envy makes us take steps to stop our neighbor having them. (*WA*, 1401, 1402)

Many writers, of many persuasions, sensing the significance of the subject, have addressed the issue. In the nineteenth century apparently there were many German proverbs on the subject of envy. As a subject of philosophy, it is worth noting that two of Nietzsche's immediate predecessors gave it special attention. The German philosopher, Immanuel Kant, in *The Metaphysics of Morals*, gives this definition of envy:

Envy (livor) is a tendency to perceive with displeasure the good of others, although it in no way detracts from one's own, and which, when it leads to action (in order to diminish that good) is called qualified envy, but otherwise only ill-will (invidentia); it is however, only an indirect malevolent frame of mind, namely a disinclination to see our own good overshadowed by the good of others, because we take its measure not from its intrinsic worth, but by comparison with the good of others and then go on to symbolize that evaluation. (*E*, 166)

Kant regarded envy as abhorrent. The German philosopher, Arthur Schopenhauer, describes envy:

[T]he soul of the alliance of mediocrity which everywhere fore-gathers instinctively and flourishes silently, being directed against individual excellence of whatever kind. For the latter is unwelcome in every individual sphere of action. . . . (*E*, 171)

Could there be any doubt that Nietzsche was indelibly influenced by these earlier thinkers? References to the problem of envy run throughout his writings. But it is in his later works that we begin to hear less about envy and more about resentment. As he examines resentment in its many forms and expressions, it becomes a central focus in his critique of Christianity. Resentment, briefly defined, usually means "an emotional response, or persistent emotional state, a feeling of displeasure, indignation, even moral outrage, resulting from a perceived slight, injury, insult, indignity, caused by some situation or event." It is usually long lasting and smoldering, and often becomes, or leads to, revenge. From his *Genealogy of Morals*, hear his words:

> All men of resentment are these physiologically distorted and worm-riddled persons, a whole quivering kingdom of burrowing revenge, indefatigable and insatiable in its outbursts against the happy, and equally so in disguises for revenge, in pretexts for revenge: when will they really reach their final, fondest, most sublime triumph of revenge? At that time, doubtless, when they succeed in pushing their own misery, indeed all misery there is, into the *consciousness* of the happy; so that the latter begin one day to be ashamed of their happiness, and perchance say to themselves when they meet, "It is a shame to be happy! *There is too much misery!*"(E, 179)

Hollingdale, in discussing Nietzsche's theory of the will to power, says this:

> What is desired, according to this theory, is the feeling of increased power. The negative aspect, that is to say the feeling of impotence, of being subject to the power of another, produces as its characteristic effect the phenomenon of *ressentiment* — and this is the chief corollary of the theory of will to power. Nietzsche developed the psychology of resentment almost as luxuriantly as he did that of power: the essence of it is that the powerless man feels resentment against those whose power he feels and against this state of powerlessness itself and out of this feeling of resentment *takes revenge* — on other people or on life itself. The objective of the revenge is to get rid of the feeling of powerlessness: the forms it takes include all moralities in which punishment is a prominent feature.... (N, 183)

In a book entitled *Envy*, by Helmut Schoeck, the author includes a discussion of the subject in the work of German philosopher, Max Scheler, a successor of Nietzsche. Schoeck writes:

> Scheler begins by explaining that the French word *ressentiment* is untranslatable, and further that Nietzsche had made of it a technical term. As such it must be retained. He believed the elements of the usual meaning of the word in French to be significant: "*Ressentiment* implies living through, and reliving, over and over, a certain emotional response reaction towards another, whereby that emotion undergoes progressive deepening and introversion into the very core of the personality, with a simultaneous distancing from the individual's sphere of expression and action." The term

further comprises the meaning that the quality of this emotion tends towards hostility. Scheler then quotes at length from Nietzsche's *Genealogy of Morality*, stressing, as that work does, that resentment is a form of self-poisoning which culminates in the vindictive impulse — What is involved is a group of emotions and affects, to which hatred, ill-will, envy, jealousy and spite also belong. . . . (E, 181)

At one point Scheler remarks: Impotent envy is also the most terrible kind of envy. Hence the form of envy which gives rise to the greatest amount of resentment is that directed against the individual and *essential being* of an unknown person: *existential envy.* For this envy, as it were, is forever muttering: "I could forgive you anything, except *that* you are, and *what* you are; except that I am not what you are; that "I," in fact am not "you." This "envy," from the start, denies the other person his very existence, which as such is most strongly experienced as "oppression" of, as "a reproach" to the person of the subject. (E, 183)

Back to Nietzsche. He asked, and needed to understand, what psychological phenomena, or process, had been the source of the morality of Christianity. His attempt at a diagnosis appears to have taken him from a consideration of envy, to that of resentment, to revenge. From his final determinations in *Ecce Homo*, hear his words:

Freedom from *ressentiment*, enlightenment over *ressentiment* — who knows the extent to which I ultimately owe thanks to my protracted sickness for this too! The problem is not exactly simple: one has to have experienced it from a state of strength and a state of weakness. If anything whatever has to be admitted against being sick, being weak, it is that in these conditions the actual curative instinct, that is to say the *defensive* and *offensive instinct* in man becomes soft. One does not know how to get free of anything, one does not know how to have done with anything, one does not know how to thrust back — everything hurts. Men and things come importunately close, events strike too deep, the memory is a festering wound. Being sick *is* itself a kind of *ressentiment.* . . . And nothing burns one up quicker than the affects of *ressentiment.* Vexation, morbid susceptibility, incapacity for revenge, poison-brewing in any sense — for one who is exhausted this is certainly the most disadvantageous kind of reaction: it causes a rapid expenditure of nervous energy, a morbid accretion of excretions, for example, of gall into the stomach. *Ressentiment* is the forbidden *in itself,* for the invalid — *his* evil: unfortunately also his most natural inclination. — This was grasped by that profound physiologist Buddha. His "religion," which one would do better to call a *system of hygiene* so as not to mix it up with such pitiable things as Christianity, makes its effect dependent on victory over *ressentiment*: to free the soul of *that* — first step to recovery. "Not by enmity is enmity ended, by friendship is enmity ended": this stands at the beginning of Buddha's teaching — it is *not* morality that speaks thus, it is physiology that speaks thus. — *Ressentiment*, born of weakness, to no one more harmful than to the weak man himself. . . . He who knows the seriousness with which my philosophy has taken up the struggle against the feelings of revengefulness and vindictiveness . . . my struggle against Christianity is only a special instance of it. (*EH*, 45, 46)

Earlier in *The Gay Science*, recall these words:

For one thing is needful: that a human being should *attain* satisfaction with himself, whether it be by means of this or that poetry and art; only then is a human being at all tolerable to behold. Whoever is dissatisfied with himself is continually ready for revenge, and we others will be his victims, if only by having to endure his ugly sight. For the sight of what is ugly makes one bad and gloomy. (*GS*, 233)

The suggestion is that the source of resentment, and of revenge, is the inability to accept oneself, to accept one's "fate." From *Thus Spoke Zarathustra*, hear his plea:

For *that man be delivered from revenge*, that is for me the bridge to the highest hope, and a rainbow after long storms. (*Z*, 99)

In one of his last books, *The Antichrist*, Nietzsche brings to a climax his many difficulties with Christianity. Here are a few of his final interpretations:

In my *Genealogy of Morals* I offered the first psychological analysis of the counter concepts of a *noble* morality and a morality of *ressentiment* — the latter born of the No to the former: but this is the Judaeo–Christian morality pure and simple. So that it could say No to everything on earth that represents the ascending tendency of life, to that which has turned out well, to power, to beauty, to self-affirmation, the instinct of *ressentiment*, which had here become genius, had to invent *another* world from whose point of view this affirmation of life appeared as evil, as the reprehensible as such. . . . (*PN*, 593)

All the concepts of the church have been recognized for what they are, the most malignant counterfeits that exist, the aim of which is to devalue nature and natural values. . . . (*PN*, 611)

In the Christian world of ideas there is nothing that has the least contact with reality — and it is in the instinctive hatred of reality that we have recognized the only motivating force at the root of Christianity. . . . One concept less, one single reality in its place — and the whole of Christianity hurtles down into nothing. . . . (*PN*, 613)

What is *bad*? But I have said this already: all that is born of weakness, of envy, of *revenge*. The anarchist and the Christian have the same origin. . . . One may posit a perfect equation between *Christian* and *anarchist*: their aim, their instinct, are directed only toward destruction. . . . (PN, 647)

The Christian church has left nothing untouched by its corruption, it has turned every value into an un-value, every truth into a lie, . . . (PN, 655)

This eternal indictment of Christianity I will write on all walls, wherever there are walls — I have letters to make even the blind see. I call Christianity the one great curse, the one great innermost corruption, the one great instinct of revenge, for which no means is poisonous, stealthy, subterranean, *small* enough — I call it the one immortal blemish of mankind. And time is reckoned from the *dies nefastus* with which this calamity began — after the first day of Christianity! *Why not rather after its last day? After today?* Revaluation of all values! (PN, 656)

CHAPTER 11. TRANSITION, EXCESS, AND PERIL

Early in his career Nietzsche wrote:

> Every deep thinker fears being understood more than he fears being misunderstood. His vanity may suffer from the latter, but his heart, his fellow-feeling suffers from the former.... (*BGE*, 230)

The final words in his last book, *Ecce Homo*:

> — Have I been understood? — *Dionysos against the Crucified....*
> (*EH*, 134)

Recall these words in *Beyond Good and Evil*:

> Everything deep loves masks; the deepest things have a veritable hatred of image and likeness. Might not *contrariety* be the only proper disguise to clothe the modesty of a god? (*BGE*, 46)

This book of mine has been a labored attempt of the *unmasking* of Nietzsche and of his "deep thinking." Here are his words in the final short chapter of *Ecce Homo*:

> The *unmasking* of Christian morality is an event without equal, a real catastrophe. He who exposes it is a *force majeure*, a destiny — he breaks the history of mankind into two parts. One lives *before* him, one lives *after* him.... (*EH*, 133)

What Nietzsche saw was German culture, European culture, Western culture, past and present, in a state of degradation and decadence. He became convinced that the primary source of this decadence, with the power to generate such a condition, was Christianity and the church, a power which it had maintained for over two thousand years. And the generating source of the power was its morality, its ability to determine moral values, those values which value *people*. And he made it understandable that the people in question were females and males. He further left little doubt that from his perspectives the defining motive behind this continuing drive for power was resentment, tending to lead to revenge. And that resentment was mainly physiological — bodies versus bodies.

Christianity had denied, redefined, reinterpreted such ideas as change, chance, uncertainty, ambiguity, life, death, sexuality, value, power, truth. Christianity had concocted a delusion — something that had been falsely believed and propagated. It had especially created the image of a god — its own "deus ex machine" — and images of man and of woman.

Nietzsche understood image making. In *The Gay Science*, these are his words:

> Someone took a youth to a sage and said: "Look, he is being corrupted by women." The sage shook his head and smiled. "It is men," said he, "that corrupt women: and all the failings of women should be atoned by and improved in men. For it is man who creates for himself the image of woman, and woman forms herself according to this image."
>
> "You are too kindhearted about women," said one of those present; "you do not know them." The sage replied: "Will is the manner of men: willingness that of women. That is the law of the sexes — truly, a hard law for women. All of humanity is innocent of its existence; but women are doubly innocent. Who could have oil and kindness enough for them?"
>
> "Damn oil! Damn kindness!" Someone else shouted out of the crowd; "Women need to be educated better!" — "Men need to be educated better," said the sage and beckoned to the youth to follow him. — The youth, however, did not follow him. (GS, 126)

Christianity had engaged in blasphemy. It had shown contempt for, irreverence toward, many things earlier considered sacred and inviolate. By means of cunning and artifice, it had invented an artificial "sacred" to reverse, cover up, or replace what is naturally sacred. Christianity had reviled and abused the natural world. Doubtless Nietzsche was familiar with the contrasting sacred symbols — the small female figures symbolizing birth and life, and the male figure on the cross symbolizing death.

Western culture was, and is, full of Christianity, defined by its moral values. Christianity continued to be the primary means, the instrument to assure the superiority and dominance of the male and assure higher value and power for a few certain males, themselves the value producers. Nietzsche believed that Christianity had been engaged in the violation of humans, a danger for both sexes. It encouraged the arrogance of power, the hubris, the abuse of power of males and of God; it encouraged weakness and obedience of females. It elevated the power/value/rank of the male and lowered the power/value/rank of the female. It separated the sexes "unnaturally," engendered hostility and violence. It encouraged an exaggerated sense of entitlement by males. The perspectives, experiences, consciousness of the male had predominated. Reduced communication between males and females resulted in men speaking with men, infrequently with women.

To borrow some words from Martin Heidegger, a devoted successor of Nietzsche's, what had long been taking place was a "one-sided view" and "one-track thinking." He called attention to the threat:

> And when man no longer sees the one side as *one* side, he has lost sight of the other side as well. (*CT*, 33)

To say that Western culture was, and is, full of Christianity, defined by its moral values — consider these words from *Ecce Homo*:

> Those things which mankind has hitherto pondered seriously are not even realities, merely imaginings, more strictly speaking *lies* from the bad instincts of sick, in the profoundest sense injurious natures — all the concepts "God," "soul," "virtue," "sin," "the Beyond," "truth," "eternal life." . . . But the greatness of human nature, its "divinity," has been sought in them. . . . All the questions of politics, the ordering of society, education have been falsified down to their foundations because the most injurious men have been taken for great men — because contempt has been taught for the "little things," which is to say for the fundamental affairs of life. . . . (*EH*, 66, 67)

Nietzsche saw clearly that these ideas, particularly the moral ideas, the values, had been successfully spread throughout Western culture. Morality — the ranking of the value of males and females — had become the structuring principle in philosophy, in art, in science, in politics, in law, in education, in medicine, in business, in the military, and in the family. Christian morality had, indeed, metastasized throughout the body of Europe, even the wider West. Nietzsche finally made no effort to conceal his horror and disgust toward those he considered the primary persons responsible for disseminating the message. In *Ecce Homo* he also wrote:

> Let us leave the possibility open that it is not mankind which is degenerating but only that parasitic species of man the *priest*, who with the aid of morality has lied himself up to being the determiner of man's values — who divines in Christian morality his means to *power*. . . . And that is my insight: the teachers, the leaders of mankind, theologians included, have also one and all been *decadents: thence* the revaluation of all values into the inimical to life, thence morality. . . . *Definition of morality*: morality — the idiosyncrasy of *decadents* with the hidden intention of *revenging themselves on life* — *and* successfully. I set store by *this* definition. (*EH*, 132, 133)

Many times, and finally once again, Nietzsche reiterated, "I am the first *immoralist*." It was not *immorality* which had poisoned the relationship between females and males — the entire Western culture — rather it was *morality*. His first definition — "morality understood as the doctrine of the rank-relations that produce the phenomenon we call 'life'" — While he was seeking a second "revaluation of all values," he rejected *all* efforts at *ranking* the sexes.

In his Foreword to *Ecce Homo*, Nietzsche says to us:

> Seeing that I must shortly approach mankind with the heaviest demand that has ever been made on it, it seems to me indispensable to say *who I am.* (*EH*, 33)

Then the opening lines of the first chapter of the same book, entitled "Why I am so Wise," reads:

> The fortunateness of my existence, its uniqueness perhaps, lies in its fatality: to express it in the form of a riddle, as my father I have already died, as my mother I still live and grow old. This twofold origin, as it were from the highest and the lowest rung of the ladder of life, at once *decadent* and *beginning* — this if anything explains that neutrality, that freedom from party in relation to the total problem of life which perhaps distinguished me. I have a subtler sense for signs of ascent and decline than any man has ever had. I am the teacher *par excellence* in this matter — I know both, I am both. My father died at the age of thirty-six: he was delicate, lovable and morbid, like a being destined to pay this world only a passing visit — a gracious reminder of life rather than life itself. . . . I now have the skill and knowledge to *invert*

perspectives: first reason why a "revaluation of values" is perhaps possible at all to me alone. — (*EH*, 38, 40)

Nietzsche, "a lover of subtleties and conundrums," has left us with the riddle that *was himself.* Should we venture a conjecture? Perhaps — he had abandoned the perspective, the thinking, the voice of the male, the father, the preacher of the artifice that was Christianity; he had retained the perspective, the thinking, the voice of the female, his young mother, the "teacher," who "read to me." He rejected the authoritarian, dogmatic voice of the father, and acquired the voice of the mother — the voice of "perhaps." Nietzsche had become a teacher, not a preacher. He remarked at one time, "I know women." He was striving to become fully engaged with life, not merely a "passing visitor." Also, he often referred to himself as a disciple of Dionysos, or as the god himself. Dionysos — frequently portrayed as the god of wine, the rose, the tree, all blossoming things, season changes; often identified with the feminine, the passions, the unconscious; whose followers were believed to be primarily women.

We should not leave without a few words regarding Nietzsche's sense of time, of his consciousness of time, which he thought had been lacking in almost all prior philosophers. As with most philosophers who came after the German philosopher Hegel (1770–1831) and his theory of historical development, Nietzsche, too, was an advocate. But of critical importance had been Bachofen and his theories of cultural history. How to understand how the past had become the present, and the present would become the future.

Cultural history, for both Bachofen and Nietzsche, could be interpreted as the evolution of human consciousness of the continuing process of the constant dynamics of the power relations between females and males, the key to which was the actual natural life process — two creative forces. Both agreed that religion has been the major instrument in defining and shaping these relationships and disseminating these models throughout the culture. As both philosopher and philologist, Nietzsche's perspectives and understanding of the *past* were derived from mythologists, historians, and philosophers. And he developed a passionate appreciation and evaluation of earlier ancient cultures. As for his *present*, we have seen in some detail that all of the evidence was

convincing — Western culture was in a state of degradation and decadence, a crisis of values. This rapidly descending loss of values — his
famous characterization of "nihilism" — was, however, accompanied
by a slowly, faintly, emerging possibility beyond nihilism. His vision of
a possible *future*, his "revaluation of all values," his "eternal recurrence"
of the same, entailed in some sense a renewal of old, very ancient values.
He believed he was a leading figure in redeeming nature, restoring to
nature its sacred character.

Many of Nietzsche's more well-known creative ideas addressed to
man were intended to give possible suggestions, or directions, to assist
in a new transcendence of the present crisis, to the future. Only briefly
— one of these was his "amor fati," love of fate. In *The Gay Science*, where
he introduced this concept, he wrote:

> Today everybody permits himself the expression of his wish and
> his dearest thought; hence I, too, shall say what it is that I wish
> from myself today, and what was the first thought to run across
> my heart this year — what thought shall be for me the reason,
> warranty, and sweetness of my life henceforth. . . . I want to learn
> more and more to see as beautiful what is necessary in things;
> then I shall be one of those who make things beautiful. *Amor fati*:
> let that be my love henceforth! I do not want to wage war against
> what is ugly. I do not want to accuse; I do not want to accuse
> those who accuse. *Looking away* shall be my only negation. And all
> in all and on the whole: some day I wish to be only a Yes-sayer.
> (*GS*, 276)

In *Ecce Homo* he adds:

> To accept oneself as a fate, not to desire oneself "different" — in
> such conditions this is *great rationality* itself. (*EH*, 47)

Another of Nietzsche's tantalizing notions is introduced in *Zarathustra's Prologue*, the overman:

> "Behold I teach you the overman. The overman is the meaning
> of the earth. Let your will say: the overman *shall be* the meaning
> of the earth! I beseech you, my brothers, *remain faithful to the earth*,
> and do not believe those who speak to you of otherworldly hopes!
> Poison-mixers are they, whether they know it or not. Despisers
> of life are they, decaying and poisoned themselves, of whom the
> earth is weary: so let them go. . . .

> "Man is a rope, tied between beast and overman — a rope over an
> abyss. A dangerous across, a dangerous on-the-way, a dangerous
> looking-back, a dangerous shuddering and stopping. (*Z*, 13, 14)

To be reminded again of this simple advice — to return the freedom, the opportunity, the responsibility, the power back to oneself. Again:

> *One thing is needful.* To "give style" to one's character — a great and rare art! It is practiced by those who survey all the strengths and weaknesses of their nature and then fit them into an artistic plan until every one of them appears as art and reason and even weaknesses delight the eye. . . . For one thing is needful: that a human being should *attain* satisfaction with himself, whether it be by means of this or that poetry and art; only then is a human being at all tolerable to behold. Whoever is dissatisfied with himself is continually ready for revenge, and we others will be his victims, if only having to endure his ugly sight. For the sight of what is ugly makes one bad and gloomy. (*GS,* 232, 233)

Creation of oneself as "beautiful," care of oneself, respect for oneself, love of oneself — these are Nietzsche's "needful things." Especially important for being "delivered from revenge."

As for the new "revaluation of all values," which Nietzsche believed was necessary, which must be undertaken following the demise of Christian values — he indicated his own point of departure. Speaking to the subject of equal rights, in *Ecce Homo* he writes:

> The more a woman is a woman the more she defends herself tooth and nail against rights in general: for the state of nature, the eternal *war* between the sexes puts her in a superior position by far. — (*EH,* 76)

Our present is part of Nietzsche's future. His influence, his power, has been well-established, and continues to spread and grow. Artists, writers, film-makers, philosophers, psychologists, theologians, scientists, critics — most bear witness to some impact of his thoughts on their own. Until Nietzsche's time, Aristotle had probably been the most influential of the philosophers. In the future, what may we predict about the influence of Nietzsche?

Nietzsche was convinced that decades, perhaps even centuries, would pass before his "time" would arrive. Perhaps now is that time. Race-consciousness, class-consciousness, national-consciousness, historical-consciousness, religious-consciousness, and gender-consciousness are rampant. Nietzsche's focus was on the latter. Also, the issues most demanding, most "thought-provoking," in our own present are the issues to which Nietzsche devoted his passion and intellect — *power, values, sexuality, religion, nature, sexual politics.* Perhaps the greatest threat to Christianity today is not atheism or secularism, but Nietzsche's naturism — reverence for, and worship of, the forces of nature. In *Ecce Homo* he wrote these words:

> The highest conception of the lyric poet was given me by *Heinrich Heine*. I seek in vain in all the realms of millennia for an equally sweet and passionate music. (*EH*, 58)

Perhaps Nietzsche had read the following by Heine:

> And she answered with a tender voice: "Let us be good friends." But what I have told you here, dear reader, that is not an event of yesterday or the day before. . . . For time is infinite, but the things in time, the concrete bodies are finite. They may indeed disperse into the smallest particles; but these particles, the atoms, have their determinate number, and the number of configurations that, all of themselves, are formed out of them is also determinate. Now, however long a time may pass, according to the eternal laws governing the combinations of this eternal play of repetition, all configurations that have previously existed on this earth must yet meet, attract, repulse, kiss and corrupt each other again. . . . And thus it will happen one day that a man will be born again, just like me, and a woman will be born, just like Mary — only that it is to be hoped that the head of this man may contain a little less foolishness — and in a better land they will meet and contemplate each other a long time; and finally the woman will give her hand to the man and say with a tender voice: "Let us be good friends." (*GS*, 16, 17)

Heidegger mentions a note Nietzsche wrote about the time of his collapse, addressed to the Dane Georg Brandes, who had delivered the first public lecture on Nietzsche at Copenhagen, in 1888. The note read:

> Postmark Torino, 4 Jan 89
>
> To my friend Georg!
> After you had discovered me, it was no trick
> To find me: the difficulty now is to lose me. . . .
> The Crucified. (*CT*, 53)

PART TWO

CHAPTER 12. THE UNIVERSE

Selecting the starting point from which to put together a reasonably coherent interpretation of the complex puzzle which is power is somewhat arbitrary and challenging. The plan, to begin with, is to fully probe as much as possible the elements in Nietzsche's thinking which may be considered as forming an interrelated, interconnected, overlapping continuum. There is also some arbitrariness, admittedly, in the sequence of examining and extending these elements. But the data are plentiful — from Nietzsche's writings, from others who probably influenced him, and from our own contemporary culture, with its increasing episodes of mind-numbing, often violent, abuses of power.

Nietzsche may be called not only a scientific philosopher, but also a philosopher of nature. He renounced earnestly any philosophy, or religion, which fashioned and promoted some additional "other" world beyond the natural world. He rejected Plato's world of ideas. And, he satirized that world and the "other" world of Christianity when he referred to the latter as "Platonism for the people." The richness of nature was more than sufficient for him — and all that existed. So, there is a natural appeal to begin this analysis and interpretation by considering his approach to power from a global perspective.

Nietzsche's philosophical and philological interests and inquiries took him back in history to the early philosophers of nature, the so-called "Pre-Socratics," to whom he was especially attracted. Mentioned earlier in the Foreword to this book, three of these appear to have figured significantly in his own development — Empedocles, Democritus, and Heraclitus. From the limited amount of information that remains of their writings, Nietzsche, nevertheless, could have taken up, and made his own, such information and ideas as these: the universe is eternal; it consists of four elements — air, earth, fire, and water — in constantly changing patterns; the defining nature of the world is "atoms, or the smallest indivisible material particles, in motion in a void"; the universe is best understood as having one controlling principle, called "Logos," which is translated as word, order, pattern, etc.; and which is revealed as pairs of opposites, which are unified by interdependence, but which exist in a state of constant strife; everything in the universe is involved in an eternal process of change and exchange.

As we explore further, it will become evident that these fragments, or nuggets of wisdom, became foundational for Nietzsche's philosophy of power and for expanding on his views. What had been emphasized by these earliest philosophers was their agreement, with varying ways of expressing their views, that motion — the eternal process of change — was the dominant feature of our natural world, plus of course, the "Logos," or "word," from Heraclitus, Nietzsche's favorite. Material bodies in constant motion, from the most minute in size to bodies of many sizes — that was the starting point. Nietzsche's focus, of course, was human bodies in motion. And his deeper thinking and analysis required an answer to the question — what is the source, or origin, of motion, all motion? Of the process of change?

Heraclitus had pointed out one kind of polar opposition — that which consists in the regular succession by one thing of its opposite, so that if one perished, so would the other. He noted, "The cold things get hot, hot gets cold, wet gets dry, dry gets damp." Or, the alternation between night and day, or sun and moon, and numerous others. The key idea for Nietzsche became, not that there are these opposites — day and night, hot and cold, wet and dry, and others, but that each one of any pair is in the continuous process of *becoming* the other. The question was how we are to understand this eternally recurring process. In the natural world this is motion, this is change. Everything in the universe is involved in the constant process of becoming. The question then was what can explain this process, and his answer was as follows:

> And do you know what "the world" is to me? Shall I show it to you in my mirror? This world: a monster of energy, without beginning, without end; an immovable, brazen enormity of energy, which does not grow bigger or smaller, which does not expend itself but only transforms itself; as a whole of unalterable size, a household without expenses or losses, but likewise without increase or income; enclosed by "nothingness" as by a boundary; not something flowing away or squandering itself, not something endlessly extended, but as a definite quantity of energy set in a definite space and not a space that might be "empty" here or there, but rather as energy throughout, as a play of energies and waves of energy at the same time one and many, increasing here and at the same time decreasing there; a sea of energies flowing and rushing together, eternally moving, eternally flooding back, with tremendous years of recurrence, with an ebb and flow of its forms; out of the simplest forms striving towards the most complex, out of the stillest, most rigid, coldest form towards the hottest, most turbulent, most self-contradictory, and then out of this abundance returning home to the simple, out of the play of contradiction back to the joy of unison, still affirming itself in the uniformity of its courses and its years, blessing itself as that which must return eternally, as a becoming that knows no repletion, no satiety, no weariness — : this is my *Dionysian* world of the eternally self-creative, the eternally self-destructive, this mystery world of the twofold delight, this my "beyond good and evil," without aim, unless the joy of the circle is itself an aim; without will, unless a ring feeling goodwill towards itself — do you want a *name* for this world? A *solution* for all your riddles? A *light* for you too, you best concealed, strongest, least dismayed, most midnight men? — *This world is the will to power* — *and nothing beside*! And you yourself are also this will to power — and nothing beside! (N, 136)

These words expressing Nietzsche's discovery, or what he might have called interpretation, are typical of much of his writing — poetic, memorable, profound. This is his controlling principle of the universe — energy, power. The implications are immeasurable. Energy — one thing, it is ubiquitous — existing everywhere at the same time. All movements, all activities, require energy. And Nietzsche gives a *name* to this energy — "the will to power." The world is the will to power. As he says, this is his definition. Life, to be alive, is to be the will to power. Man is the will to power. And this was his focus — the human being, constantly changing, in motion, becoming. Not atoms in motion, as Democritus had suggested, but bodies in motion — and most importantly, human bodies. And human bodies present themselves in multiple, indeterminate motions, or activities.

Recall — the seventeenth century philosopher, Thomas Hobbes, as we saw earlier, took the position that all men continuously desire power and more power until death. This is what it means to be a living human being. Hobbes also addressed briefly the idea of motion, perhaps influencing Nietzsche's thinking. Hobbes wrote:

> There be in animals two sorts of *motions* peculiar to them: one called *vital*, begun in generation and continued without interruption through their whole life — such as are the *course* of the *blood*, the *pulse*, the *breathing*, the *concoction, nutrition, excretion*, etc. — to which motions there needs no help of imagination, otherwise called *voluntary motion* — as to *go*, to *speak*, to *move* any of our limbs in such a manner as is first fancied in our minds. (*AE*, 174)

Nietzsche's "will to power" is a natural impulse, a drive, a feeling, a need to discharge, express, exercise, increase this energy. It is ambiguous. Humans constantly experience this process, these motions, change, power in different forms, different ever-shifting patterns. All human activity is infused with this drive for power, for the "feeling of power." Nietzsche urged us to experiment with the idea that the will to power could explain *all* human activities. And those activities which he obviously considered fundamental were those of the five senses — sight, sound, taste, smell, and touch. Or, the eyes, ears, mouth, nose, and hands. All of these are active in having access to the world in which humans are participants, in the universe of change, process, becoming. They are the physiological aspects of human bodies, the powers, abilities, which enable humans in constantly engaging this enormous, ubiquitous, constantly changing world — natural and cultural. Nietzsche's passion, his intellect, and his wit pursued with vigor what is often referred to merely as "sense experience." He thought, and wrote, about all of the senses, but perceiving had by far most of his attention. And as with all of his ideas, the point of reference was always power.

CHAPTER 13. PERCEPTION AND KNOWLEDGE

Analyzing, or interpreting, the experience of perceiving had long been considered by philosophers as the ground, the beginning, the foundation of knowledge, of truth — even as far back in the Western tradition as the Pre-Socratics. They reminded us that we perceive something which is called air, something called earth, something called fire, and something called water. We also perceive — each according to the name which it has been given — change, process, becoming, motion, multiple pairs of opposites — and more.

The unexamined assumption apparently had been that things in the external world are constantly moving and changing, but that there is one fixed viewpoint, one standpoint — a position from which objects or principles are perceived. Nietzsche stated unequivocally that men no longer believe this. And, as with most, perhaps all, of those ideas which were considered essential to the ideology of Western thinking, he exploded this assumption, and developed his own position.

The activity of perceiving retained its preeminent position — it is the beginning, the ground, of what we call knowledge. Immediate sensory experience — primarily perception — is our way of being constantly engaged with both ourselves and what is other than ourselves. The idea used frequently by Nietzsche, and later interpreters, was that

of phenomenon — any fact, event, situation, external or internal, usually involving the senses.

Nietzsche's radically new way of interpreting perception was that
all perception, every act of perceiving, is *perspectival*. Not only do we
perceive motion and change, but also the body of the perceiving individual, the eyes, are continually moving, or capable of moving, of exercising the ability, the power, to have multiple, indefinite perspectives.
There is not one single perspective, no "right" perspective, no "wrong"
perspective. There are infinite perspectives, and every one is subjective
and relative to the perceiving individual. Nietzsche wrote:

> [T]oday we are at least far from the ridiculous immodesty that
> would be involved in decreeing from our corner that perspectives
> are permitted only from this corner. Rather has the world become
> "infinite" for us all over again, inasmuch as we cannot reject the
> possibility that *it may include infinite interpretations*. (*GS*, 336)

This change — *perspectivism* — was revolutionary, and implied com-
plexity that remains far from being understood. The ability to perceive
is a formidable natural power, a major function of living bodies. The
experience of perceiving, this activity, is undoubtedly interconnected
with many other experiences, possibly to all of the experiences which
constitute what we call "life." After this idea of perspectivism was recognized and affirmed, our ways of knowing and understanding would
never be the same. Some of the basic questions apply — where, when,
what, and particularly *who*?

Considering many other of his so-called "reversals," when Nietzsche
suggested that at his time and place, he alone had the ability to invert
his perspectives, it is possible, even probable, that he was referring to
two very different ways of perceiving. Male experience and female experience — physiological, psychological, social, etc. — are very different, as Nietzsche understood. He may well have been saying that in addition to his own perspectives, he had the ability to perceive the world
from a very different point of view — that of the female. And to think
and understand differently. No more "one-sided view" and "one-track
thinking." That changed his perspectival possibilities exponentially.
The process which is perceiving may be significantly different for the
female and the male. And everything about you and your life depends
upon your perspectives — those constantly changing perspectives.

With such an explosive revisioning of the phenomenon of perception, another change was in the offing. If all knowledge begins with sense perception — as has been widely accepted in philosophical communities — how did this notion of perspective affect the idea of knowledge? What is it that is called "knowledge"? And, of course, Nietzsche segued right into what necessarily would follow — another shocker — a revolutionary revision of the idea of knowledge.

All knowledge is *interpretation* of experience, especially experiences of the senses, particularly the experience of perceiving. And, in Nietzsche's thinking, there are always multiple, unlimited, indefinite interpretations. The activity of interpreting is that of explaining, or better, that of giving meaning to phenomena. And we should not forget that Nietzsche often reminded us to not forget — that *ambiguity* is a constituent, an essential part, or characteristic, of the very process, or activity, of interpreting.

Ubiquity was the watchword when Nietzsche was speaking about the universe and energy, or power. Ambiguity is the watchword when he is speaking about interpretation. Obviously, interpretations are a major means to power, to the feeling of power for oneself, to the exercise of power in relating to others. As with perceiving, interpreting is subjective, and relative to the interpreting person. Nietzsche realized that knowledge, i.e., interpretation — in any area, everywhere — is power. He considered each of the major sciences and ended with this:

> Today it is dawning on perhaps five or six minds that physics, too, is only an interpretation of the universe, an arrangement of it (to suit us, if I may be so bold!) (*BGE*, 15)

And interpretations are formed and communicated through words — spoken and written.

Chapter 14. Words

To venture into the world of words is like stepping into quicksand. And, if one is Heraclitean by persuasion, it is like entering the world of the wars. One needs, at the very least, to carry along a good dictionary. For Nietzsche, this *was* his world. For him — loving words, hating words; fearing words, but courageous in the encounter with words; collecting and treasuring words, and discarding others; creating and destroying words. Words, indeed, were for him, his toys, his tools, his weapons.

And, the word around which all others seemed to revolve was *power*. The challenge was to understand the word itself. But more captivating was the irresistible need, the desire, the demand to explore the territory of the *power of words*. This was the puzzle of a lifetime.

Nietzsche told us that one of three most important "small" things for every individual life was what one does for recreation; the other two were nutrition, and location and climate, or where one lived or spent most of their time. The latter two must await another time for further elaboration. However, as for his recreation, he says that, for him, it was reading. But reading was for only part of the time. A large part was given to thinking, speaking, and writing. Words in, words out.

Nietzsche was educated as a classical philologist, and taught classical philology for a brief time in Basel. His academic reading would have included Greek historians — Herodotus and Thucycides; Greek poets — Hesiod and Homer; Greek dramatists — Aeschylus, Sophocles, and Euripides and Aristophanes, writer of comedy; and of course, Greek philosophers — the Pre-Socratics, Socrates, Plato, and Aristotle. These were all writers of words, and their words had been taken as forming the basic structure of Western culture. They had endured for centuries. It was the power, i.e., the ability of these men to think, and write these words. Also, the words themselves had retained, at times increased, their own power, i.e., force, strength. Of course, Nietzsche was also a student of the Old and New Testaments.

Part One of this book explored Nietzsche's interpretation and response to these words — words written and spoken by men and the power these words had carried for a very long time. The words which were Christianity were beginning to lose their force, and Nietzsche was determined to show, from his perspectives, why this was so. And his intention was to use his own power of words to contest and demolish those of religion.

One of the most exciting and revolutionary aspects of Nietzsche's thinking was this. We are constantly perceiving material things, bodies in motion, undergoing change, but of more recent times humans began perceiving different "things" — words. And hearing more of them. We were beginning to become conscious of words, of the power of words. Recall this brief quotation of Nietzsche's. He said, "The Germans invented gunpowder — all credit to them! But they made up for it by inventing the printing press."

Man was always participating in the ubiquity of energy. Increasingly, at least for Nietzsche, the use of words in the activity of speaking was being understood as the power that it is. And not only were they everywhere, all of the time, words share in the pervasive ambiguity of which he often reminded his readers. In investigating the power of words, of speaking, it is necessary to use words — especially questions. What is power? What is called "power"? Who names power? Who has the power of naming power? Who is called "powerful"? Nietzsche, and we, are confronting a dizzying array of questions. But throughout his life spent writing, the subject, or questions, revolved around the individual — *who?* And one important way of looking at his thinking is in recognizing that these three ideas formed a threesome — the *person*, *power*, and *words*.

Not money, not armaments, not oil — rather, words and the powers that attach to words. That is the treasure of individuals and communities — the power of perceiving words, listening to words, and speaking words. It has been suggested that the decay of language is the decay of man.

Nietzsche was aware that the words traditionally had belonged to mythologists, historians, philosophers, theologians, literary artists, scientists, politicians, militarists. These were the "who" of the past, those who exercised and expressed power, who were in control, often in conflict among themselves.

To the questions — what is power?, or, what is called "power"?, the concept embraces many terms. There is a large family of terms, and the dictionary is the immediate and direct access. What follows is a short scan of the words which are part of this web. These are frequently listed as some of the primary meanings: the ability to do or act; the capability of doing or accomplishing something; strength, might, force; possession of control or command over others — minds or bodies; authority; rule; influence; energy; momentum. Associated with these are inspire, spur, sustain, urge, persuade, move, induce, entice, give power to, make powerful, empower. The original focus of Nietzsche appears to have been on the term "energy." And from the dictionary — physical energy, (especially physics), mechanical energy, electrical energy, atomic energy, nuclear energy, computer energy. And the power of numbers — mathematics.

The entanglements among these various terms, or meanings, are further confusing. One term may be defined by another. We find such phrases as "the force of authority." There are numerous similar combinations. The terms, or meanings, often come in different grammatical forms — energy, energize, energetic, energetically, etc. The word "power" is frequently used as the first part of a two-part word — power play, power base, power cable, power house, power structure, and more.

The concept "power" — and the words with which we speak about power — plus the expressions and exercises of power which are perceived and experienced in constantly shifting patterns — give credence to Nietzsche's interpretation of the universe. It is a "monster of energy" — characterized by ubiquity and ambiguity.

Of special interest to Nietzsche, and to later students of language, was the use and power of words in the activity of "naming." Recall these words of his:

> *Only as creators!* — This has given me the greatest trouble and still does: to realize that what things *are called* is   incomparably more important than what they are. The reputation, name, and appearance, the usual measure and weight of a thing, what it counts for — originally almost always wrong and arbitrary, thrown over things like a dress and altogether foreign to their nature and even to their skin — all this grows from generation unto generation, merely because people believe in it, until it gradually grows to be part of the thing and turns into its very body. What at first was appearance becomes in the end, almost invariably, the essence and is effective as such. How foolish it would be to suppose that one only needs to point out this origin and this misty shroud of delusion in order to *destroy* the world that counts for real, so-called *"reality."* We can destroy only as creators. — But let us not forget this either: it is enough to create new names and estimations and probabilities in order to create in the long run new "things." (*BGE*, 121, 122)

Nietzsche named energy "the will to power." He named morality:

> — morality understood as the doctrine of rank-relations that produce the phenomenon we call "life." — (*BGF*, 22)

And then he named himself "an immoralist." He named Immanuel Kant "old Tartuffery." Nietzsche was constantly naming, renaming, creating new names, defining and redefining — seriously and in jest. He reinterpreted the process and significance of naming. Changing the name of a thing, or changing the thing to which a name applies — that is power. Naming, renaming, or changing the names of persons is possibly more powerful. To mention, or identify, a person by name, by the use of a word or phrase, especially in describing or defining in a disparaging fashion, is an exercise of power. The person "becomes" the name. Name-calling, the use of offensive names, especially in the attempt to win an argument or to induce rejection or condemnation of a person is part of the daily discourse of politics — and powerful. Consider the pseudonym — a fictitious or false name. Traditionally, the woman has changed her name and assumed the name of the man. And the renaming changes her identity, often significantly. And nicknames? Naming is a frequent stratagem in the discourse of politics. "Dirty bomber," "illegal enemy combatant," "terrorist" are examples. "Hero," "victim," "collateral damage" — familiar instances of naming, and the power of naming.

And what about the symbolic use of words? One needs a different type of dictionary. Many words, along with their often visual counterparts, represent power. Hair, for example, or fire, or mouth. These representations are too numerous to explore. But they fascinated Nietzsche. They offered an entirely new wealth of possibilities — of power. He changed forever the ways in which we perceive, interpret, appreciate, evaluate words. The word is "power."

A postscript — the wisdom of the individuals who created this nation, the so-called "Founding Fathers," was the wisdom, the understanding, that the power of a newly-born and developing nation, like the power of a newly-born and developing person, was the power of words — of speaking and writing. Their wisdom was in understanding the power and their added ability, or power, of using, expressing, exercising these powers. Ultimately, not bayonets, not bullets — not bombs had they been available — would prevail. So, they wrote the *Declaration of Independence* and the *Constitution of the United States of America*. It is not surprising that the first of the ten Amendments to the Constitution, which became the Bill of Rights, recognized and named as their primary concern, the protection of the power and privilege of speech and religion. They understood well the power of words, and in particular, the power of words within the context of religion. I think we may interpret those words, and the priority of giving voice to those issues, as evidence that these individuals were saying that religious words and speaking were to be protected, but also that of all forms of discourse, religious words probably provided the greatest threat and danger to the young republic.

Almost a century later, Nietzsche developed his critique of Christianity on the evidence that he interpreted similarly, and extensively.

CHAPTER 15. CONTRARIES

Nietzsche, as a classical philologist — the lover of learning and literature — in discovering the language of symbols and myths, was also learning the words, few as they were, of the early, ancient philosophers. And his particular favorite was Heraclitus. The mythologists, in the language of symbols, and Heraclitus, in the language of natural philosophy, were both focusing their attention on the same idea, one "controlling principle." Heraclitus called it "Logos," which is translated variously as word, order, pattern, etc. This pattern is revealed as pairs of opposites, contraries which are unified by interdependence, but which Heraclitus also believed existed in a state of constant conflict. Everything in the universe is involved in an eternal process of change and exchange. This is motion, to which Nietzsche added the notion of energy, of power, to account for the motion. Recall these words from Nietzsche:

> When one speaks of *humanity*, the idea is fundamental that this is something which separates and distinguishes man from nature. In reality, however there is no such separation: "natural" qualities and those called truly "human" are inseparately grown together. Man, in his highest and noblest capacities, is wholly nature and embodies its uncanny dual character. (*PN*, 32)

I interpreted this "uncanny dual nature" of all living things in nature as meaning the pair — male and female. Nature — for the mythologist, for Heraclitus, and for Nietzsche — provides the primary, initial evidence. We perceive these opposites everywhere, all of the time. And in nature, the most obvious, the model, and most important in human experience, is female and male — bodies. Human culture reflects this "Logos" — in words, symbols, and visual images.

If there is any doubt as to the impact of these ideas on Nietzsche's thinking, then reconsider these words:

> Everything deep loves masks; the deepest things have a veritable hatred of image and likeness. Might not *contrariety* be the only proper disguise to clothe the modesty of a god? A question worth asking. It would be surprising if some mystic hadn't at some time ventured upon it. There are events of such delicate nature that one would do well to bury them in gruffness and make them unrecognizable. . . . Such a concealed one, who instinctively uses speech for silence and withholding, and whose excuses for not communicating are inexhaustible, *wants* and encourages a mask of himself to wander about in the hearts and minds of his friends. And if he doesn't want it, one day his eyes will be opened to the fact that the mask is there anyway, and that it is good so. Every thinker needs a mask; even more, around every deep thinker a mask constantly grows, thanks to the continually wrong, i.e. superficial, interpretations of his every word, his every step, his every sign of life. — (*BGE*, 46, 47)

It may appear excessive, or untidy, calling attention to some of the pairs of opposites which stand out in Nietzsche's thinking. However, in no particular order, here are several: male/female, creative/destructive, self/other, benefit/harm, possibility/ impossibility, sickness/health, attraction/aversion, active/passive, heat/cold, affirm/deny, increase/ decrease, ascend/descend, good/evil, life/death, same/different, truth/ error, truth/lie, hard/soft, command/obey, strength/weakness, friend/ enemy, beginning/end, superior/inferior, permanence/change, abilities/ inabilities, subjective/objective, beautiful/ugly, appearance/reality — and many more.

Some opposites are based within nature and sense experience, and also found their way into mythology. Examples are: night/day, sun/ moon, left/right — and more. Nietzsche learned that many of these pairs used symbolically, referred to female and male. He, teasingly perhaps, made up a few of his own. "Supposing that Truth is a woman —." Also, "Life is a woman." Or, "Justice is a woman."

It should be noted that there were a few pairs of opposites which Nietzsche rejected as artificial, inappropriate, invented, misapplied, false. The pair, beginning and end, was one. While it was appropriate in many situations, in many events, in a single life, it was not applicable in speaking of the beginning and the end in referring to the universe — neither in philosophical nor theological discourse. Immanuel Kant recognized that. Also for Nietzsche, to cast body and soul as opposites was an invention, or false. Since he argued that the soul, either in Platonic thought or Christian thought, was an invention and false, it had no legitimacy in the context of opposites. As we will see later, only the body exists and the soul is "something about the body." As for heaven and hell, they were both fictitious inventions — useful in the power of Christianity — extensions of pleasure and pain, as well as reward and punishment.

A brief commentary on some of the contraries important to Nietzsche seems worthwhile. If throughout his life, the subjects, and his questions, revolved around the individual person, then we may take as the lead pair of opposites — again, male and female — the basis of life in nature. That has been, and will continue to be, the focus of this book. As for creative and destructive — those also are clearly original in nature. The two powers — in the air, the fire, the earth, and the water — and in that part of nature which is humanity. Nietzsche was never unaware that his thinking and his words were spoken to accomplish both — to destroy old ways of thinking and to create new ones. He understood that humans, in the exercise of the will to power, in life, all participated in power in creating and destroying.

Another important pair shows up in the early development of his thinking regarding power. Recall these words:

> *On the doctrine of the feeling of power.* — Benefiting and hurting others are ways of exercising one's power over others; that is all one desires in such cases. One hurts those whom one wants to feel one's power, for pain is a much more efficient means to that end than pleasure; pain always raises the question about its origin while pleasure is inclined to stop with itself without looking back. . . . Certainly the state in which we hurt others is rarely as agreeable, in an unadulterated way, as that in which we benefit others; it is a sign that we are still lacking power, or it shows a sense of frustration in the face of this poverty; it is accompanied by new dangers and uncertainties for what power we do possess, and clouds

our horizon with the prospect of revenge, scorn, punishment and failure. (*GS*, 86, 87)

Important in Nietzsche's experience was the fact that he had frequent episodes of becoming ill, followed by recovery, and then the reversal. He often recounted the decrease and increase in his energy and ability — his powers — that were vividly part of this recurring process. Like night and day, sickness and health were part of life, as were pain and pleasure, joy and sorrow, and so much more. One did not have the health and not the sickness, the pleasure and not the pain, the joy and not the sorrow. Having both was a *necessity*; one without the other was never a possibility of nature, of life.

When Nietzsche claimed, or proclaimed, that his chosen principle to inform his life was "Amor Fati," his many dissenters found good reasons to disagree. In his view, to affirm one's fate, or destiny, to love rather than hate life, meant to affirm everything, including one's own situation in the universe. This, for him, meant fully and completely. Nature, life, the body — all were sacred and worthy of affirmation, love, and devotion. And a person could choose either to affirm or deny this life. Could he have said it better than this?

> *For the new year.* — I still live, I still think: I still have to live, for I still have to think. *Sum, ergo cogito: cogito, ergo sum*. Today everybody permits himself the expression of his wish and his dearest thought; hence I, too, shall say what it is that I wish from myself today, and what was the first thought to run across my heart this year — what thought shall be for me the reason, warranty, and sweetness of my life henceforth. I want to learn more and more to see as beautiful what is necessary in things; then I shall be one of those who make things beautiful. *Amor fati*; let that be my love henceforth! I do not want to wage war against what is ugly! I do not want to accuse; I do not even want to accuse those who accuse. *Looking away* shall be my only negation. And all in all and on the whole: some day I wish to be only a Yes-sayer. (*GS*, 223)

As for the opposites good and evil, they became the title of one of Nietzsche's most popular books, *Beyond Good and Evil*. The title should suggest that perhaps his interpretation of this pair of contraries was not in agreement with conventional usage and understanding. As we will see later when discussing more thoroughly the subject of values, and as is the case with all values, good and evil are not qualities, or characteristics, that are inherent in individuals or actions. They are subjective and relative to the observer, interpreter, or speaker. Also, good and evil are not abstract entities in themselves. One would need to read his book to understand the many perspectives which he takes in such an expanded and revolutionary interpretation. Humans create or invent these, apply them, and as the title of the book implies, must transcend them in favor of other values — part of his anticipated enterprise of the "revaluation of all values."

As a pair of opposites, same and different was one of those which interested Heraclitus — the experience of stepping into the same river, but simultaneously into ever-changing different waters. These contraries, which Nietzsche explores in several ways, become wonderfully fruitful in his somewhat oblique addressing of what I will refer to as the question of "identity" later in this discussion.

As for the opposites hard and soft, Nietzsche uses these as symbols — perhaps gleaned from mythological sources, or perhaps from his own imagination. I have interpreted the following short story as a parable, a fable, or perhaps an allegory:

> "Why so hard?" the kitchen coal once said to the diamond. "After all, are we not close kin?" Why so soft? O my brothers, thus I ask you: are you not after all my brothers? Why so soft, so pliant and yielding? Why is there so much denial, self-denial, in your hearts? So little destiny in your eyes? And if you do not want to be destinies and inexorable ones, how can you one day triumph with me? And if your hardness does not wish to flash and cut and cut through, how can you one day create with me?

> For creators are hard. And it must seem blessedness to you to impress your hand on millennia as on wax. Blessedness to write on the will of millennia as on bronze — harder than bronze, nobler than bronze. Only the noblest is altogether hard. This new tablet, O my brothers, I place over you: *become hard!* (Z, 214)

These symbols hard and soft offer the persuasive possibility that Nietzsche was referring to male and female, to future creators of a new "table of values," the "revaluation of all values," which became increasingly important for him.

One of the meanings most often associated with power is that of command, with its opposite obey, or obedience. And most often it is understood as having power over others. Of course, Nietzsche recognized, and believed, that some individuals had the natural capability, or ability, to command to a greater degree than some others. But his emphasis was on the possibility that individuals could, and should, stress the exercise of that power in regard to themselves. He seems to be suggesting that strengthening awareness and developing this capability, this type or expression of power, is a great source of self-respect, of self-affirmation.

The distinction between appearance and reality had traditionally been a pair of opposites of major significance in philosophy, especially since it was the basis of Plato's theory of forms or ideas, and in Nietzsche's view, had been the origin of, or at least the support of, the later notion in Christianity of another world of perfection. Nietzsche dissolved that opposition, considering it an error, if not a falsehood. He wrote about this many times. In his Foreword to *Ecce Homo*, he wrote this:

> I am, for example, absolutely not a bogey-man, not a moral-monster — I am even an antithetical nature to the species of man hitherto honoured as virtuous. Between ourselves, it seems to me that precisely this constitutes part of my pride. I am a disciple of the philosopher Dionysos, I prefer to be even a satyr rather than a saint. But you have only to read this writing. Perhaps I have succeeded in giving expression to this antithesis in a cheerful and affable way — perhaps this writing had no point at all other than to do this. The last thing *I* would promise would be to "improve" mankind. I erect no new idols; let the old idols learn what it means to have legs of clay. *To overthrow idols* (my word for "ideals") — that rather is my business. Reality has been deprived of its value, its meaning, its veracity to the same degree as an ideal world has been *fabricated*. . . . The "real world" and the "apparent world" — in plain terms: the *fabricated* world and reality. . . . The *lie* of the ideal has hitherto been the curse on reality, through it mankind itself has become mendacious and false down to its deepest instincts — to the point of worshipping the *inverse* values to those which alone could guarantee it prosperity, future, the exalted *right* to a future. (*EH*, 33, 34)

We know that Nietzsche proclaimed, and loudly, that there is this world, only one. He set about to redeem nature, life, the body, sexuality. It may be claimed that beyond any other individual thinker, Nietzsche grasped the richness of our world. There are unlimited perspectives, unlimited interpretations, unlimited words, and unlimited pairs of opposites. A staggering set of revelations!

CHAPTER 16. BODY AND BODIES

What is called "body"? Let's begin with these two definitions — (1) the organized physical substance of an animal or plant either living or dead, and (2) the material part or nature of a human being. From the earliest evidence that is accessible, in myths, in drawings, whatever, it is clear that the representations always were centered on human bodies — in motion. Nietzsche, being of the nineteenth century, once slightly ridiculed Democritus for emphasizing atoms, the smallest indivisible material bodies in motion, as the fundamental and defining nature of the universe. For Nietzsche, understanding the energy, the powers of the *human body* had always been, was, and would continue to be, the dominating concern of humans. Human bodies are the primary objects of sense experiences, of interpretations, of words, of oppositions, and until death, are the primary natural objects in motion — at least from the perspectives of humans. The experiences of human bodies, by human bodies, is central. The idea of change, of process, of becoming, however universally extended, remains ultimately on persons — the human animal.

As was noted in the first part of this book, the seventeenth century English philosopher, Thomas Hobbes, largely influenced by conflicts both civil and religious, contributed substantially to our understanding of power, and the important position power holds in examining man's nature, as well as in civil and political contexts. And as we claimed earlier, he probably influenced Nietzsche's thinking regarding power. But Hobbes, as was Nietzsche, was deeply influenced by the new physical theories developed by Galileo and others. And he developed his own natural philosophy around the ideas of matter in motion, or bodies in motion. In his *Leviathan*, Hobbes wrote this:

> There be in animals two sorts of *motions* peculiar to them: one called *vital*, begun in generation and continued without interruption through their whole life — such as are the *course* of the *blood*, the *pulse*, the *breathing*, the *concoction, nutrition, excretion*, etc. — to which motions there needs no help of imagination; the other is *animal motion*, otherwise called *voluntary motion* — as to *go*, to *speak*, to *move* any of our limbs in such manner as is first fancied in our minds. (*AE*, 174)

It appears that Hobbes was one of the earliest modern philosophers to give some thought to the human body, to the activities, the motions and processes of the body. He was becoming interested in the new science of physiology — a branch of biology that deals with the functions and activities of life, or of living matter, and of the physical and chemical phenomena involved. Physiology is concerned with the organic processes and phenomena of an organism or any of its parts, or of a particular bodily process. Hobbes also was beginning to give attention to another emerging science, psychology, considering for example, the two motions, attraction and aversion.

Nietzsche's interests favored both sciences — physiology and psychology — and he referred to himself as a "physiological psychologist." Man was entirely body, and all activities were bodily activities, expressing that energy, that will to power. Like other "idols," Nietzsche redefined, or reinterpreted, the "soul" of Plato and of Christianity. There is no separate, immaterial soul, only activities of the mind, which is part of the body. Mental activities, motions, processes — like those of the senses — are bodily. He wrote this:

> The unconscious disguise of physiological needs under the cloaks of the objective, ideal, purely spiritual goes to frightening lengths — and often I have asked myself whether, taking a large view, philosophy has not been merely an interpretation of the body and a *misunderstanding of the body*. (*GS*, 34, 35)

He also wrote this:

> By putting an end to the superstitions hitherto almost tropi-
> cally rampant around the ideas of soul, the *new* psychologist has
> pushed himself out, as it were, into new barrenness and new sus-
> picions. It may be that the older psychologists had a jollier and
> more comfortable time — but in the end the new psychologist
> has sentenced himself to new inventions — and who knows? —
> perhaps new discoveries! (*BGE*, 14, 15)

And in *Thus Spoke Zarathustra*, these words:

> I want to speak to the despisers of the body. I would not have
> them learn and teach differently, but merely say farewell to their
> own bodies — and thus become silent.

> "Body am I, and soul" — thus speaks the child. And why should
> one not speak like children?

> But the awakened and knowing say: body am I entirely, and
> nothing else; and soul is only a word for something about the
> body. (*Z*, 34)

You do not *have* a body, you *are* your body. "I," "self," refer to one's
material body. Like the idea of another world, the "soul" has been an
invention, a fabrication. In Nietzsche's thinking, only one world — the
natural world, and only the body, in this life, no other.

As a cultural historian and critic, the significance of the body in
ancient cultures, prior to the time of Plato, became of special interest
to Nietzsche. These early cultures gave every indication that the body,
the powers of the body, and the celebration of those powers, were
paramount. Nietzsche referred to himself as a disciple of Dionysus, to
the Dionysian spirit and festivals. The value placed on nature and the
natural body contrasted sharply with the philosophical and religious
disvalue of both during his time. Recall this:

> What is astonishing about the religiosity of the ancient Greeks
> is the lavish abundance of gratitude that radiates from it. Only a
> very distinguished type of human being stands in *that* relation to
> nature and to life. Later, when the rabble came to rule in Greece,
> *fear* choked out religion and prepared the way for Christianity.
> (*BGE*, 58)

Plato famously invented the soul, valued the soul, devalued the
body. But interestingly, another form of denigration/celebration of the
body was widespread in Greece before and during the time of Plato
— wars, the extreme form of aggression, competition, conflict, and
death. However, there were the Olympic Games, an innovative and

grand celebration of the body — its astonishing energy and abilities, its powers.

From celebration and positive valuation of the body by the ancients, to "misunderstanding of the body" by philosophers, to denial and crushing devaluation of the body by Christianity — that appears to be the historical process as Nietzsche interpreted it. The Renaissance, with its vigorous artistic and intellectual activity, and the humanistic revival of Classical influences, brought a revival and revaluation of the body, particularly in the arts, and in the sciences.

Nietzsche aligned himself on the side of art and science and against the powers of Christianity and the church. Devaluation, denigration, decay, destruction of the body versus valuation, celebration, protection, creation of the body, with all of its marvelous powers — those were contraries, the choices. That was the substance of the "war" to which Nietzsche devoted his life, his powers. When he referred to himself as "a warrior," and celebrated the warrior, it was to enlist in the war of words, not the war of bullets and bombs. Or, perhaps also in the war between the words of the ancient Greeks and those of Christianity — "revaluation of all values," of nature, life, the body. He was a Dionysian, or the modern Dionysos himself.

The perspectives on the species had identified and interpreted the human body as similar to, but different from, other living bodies. The two leading voices in the West, speaking of the differences between the two types of bodies — male and female — were Aristotle and Thomas Aquinas. They provided the damaging duet, proclaiming that the female body was a "misbegotten," inferior form. Philosophy and Christian theology dominated Western thinking for centuries. But the artists of the Renaissance were reviving, particularly in visual imagery, the beauty, the grace, the splendors, the awe-inspiring forms and powers of bodies. And there were *two* forms — same and different, female and male. The emerging new sciences — biology, anatomy, physiology, medicine — were forced to recognize these physical differences. And the primary and defining difference, as the artists were revealing was the sexual body — sexuality. Nietzsche, the "scientific philosopher," often hoped for, or saw on the horizon, what he called "medico-philosophers."

Nietzsche could not have avoided being born into the dynamic artistic and intellectual environment. As a philosopher, as a classical philologist, and as a mythologist, he was drawn to the new science of psychology. He referred to himself as a "physio-psychologist," and wrote these words:

> A proper physio-psychology must battle with unconscious resistances in the heart of the investigator; his "heart" sides against it. . . . But imagine someone who takes the very passions — hatred, envy, greed, domineering — to be the passions upon which life is conditioned, as things which must be present in the total household of life. Takes them to be necessary in order to preserve the very nature of life, to be further developed if life is to be further developed! Such a man suffers from the inclination of his judgment as though from seasickness! But even this hypothesis is by no means the most painful or the strangest in this enormous, almost totally unknown domain of dangerous insights. Indeed, there are a hundred good reasons for staying away from it if one — can! On the other hand, if our ship has once taken us there — very well, let us go ahead, grit our teeth, open our eyes, grip the rudder and — ride out morality! Perhaps we will crush and destroy our own remaining morality, but do *we* matter! Never yet has a *deeper* world of insight been opened to bold travellers and adventurers. And the psychologist who can make this sort of "sacrifice" (it is not the *sacrifizio dell' intelletto* — on the contrary!) will be at least in a position to demand that psychology be acknowledged once more as the mistress of the sciences, for whose service and preparation the other sciences exist. For psychology is now again the road to the basic problems. (*BGE*, 26, 27)

The basic sense of contrariety in nature was the irreducible dualism of two different types of bodies, unified by interdependence, but which (if one is inclined to be of Heraclitean persuasion) exist in a state of constant strife. Or, if inclined to be of Democritean persuasion, as was Nietzsche in the case of the sexes, in a state, or process, of constantly changing between love and strife. Nietzsche appears to have had no doubt that this dualism was necessary and universal. In his view, this must be recognized and made the first principle of every science. It was obvious to him that this was the case, especially within the sciences of physiology and psychology. Let's suggest some differences which perhaps are fundamental — experiences, sense perceptions and perspectives, interpretations, tastes, needs, voices, memories, imaginations, consciousness of change, process, becoming. And for Nietzsche especially differences in powers or abilities, and values.

The two major differences, I would offer, are those of experience and change. In females and males, the significance of these two differences, and the perception, appreciation, and evaluation of them are critical. The cultural convulsions of our present time, and forecast by Nietzsche, perhaps are due in large part to our rapidly expanding consciousness of our similarities, but especially of our differences. This is gender-consciousness. If one is inclined to be of Nietzschean persuasion, these are inextricably related to the will to power, the impulse or drive for power. This is gender politics. And, as we will consider in the next chapter, being either male or female is fundamental to the issue of *identity*.

Chapter 17. Identity

The subtitle of one of Nietzsche's last books, *Ecce Homo*, is *How One Becomes What One Is*. The suggestion of advice, or instruction, seems to be regarding how one develops one's capabilities or potentialities. The Foreword to the book then begins:

> Seeing that I must shortly approach mankind with the heaviest demand that has ever been made on it, it seems to me indispensable to say *who I am*. (*EH*, 33)

Immediately following the Foreword Nietzsche writes this prose poem:

> On this perfect day, when everything has become ripe and not only the grapes are growing brown, a ray of sunlight has fallen on to my life: I looked behind me, I looked before me, never have I seen so many and such good things together. Not in vain have I buried my forty-fourth year today, I was *entitled* to bury it — what there was of life in it is rescued, is immortal. The first book of the *Revaluation of all Values*, the *Songs of Zarathustra*, the Twilight of the Idols, my attempt to philosophize with a hammer — all of them gifts of this year, of its last quarter even! *How should I not be grateful to my whole life?* — And so I tell myself my life. (*EH*, 37)

Then he begins the first chapter of the book, entitled "Why I Am So Wise," with these words:

> The fortunateness of my existence, its uniqueness perhaps, lies in its fatality: to express it in the form of a riddle, as my father I have already died, as my mother I still live and grow old. This

twofold origin, as it were from the highest and the lowest rung of the ladder of life, at once *decadent* and *beginning* — this if anything explains that neutrality, that freedom from party in relation to the total problem of life which perhaps distinguishes me. I have a subtler sense for signs of ascent and decline than any man has ever had, I am the teacher *par excellence* in this matter — I know both, I am both. — My father died at the age of thirty-six: he was delicate, lovable and morbid, like a being destined to pay this world only a passing visit — a gracious reminder of life rather than life itself. In the same year in which his life declined mine too declined: in the thirty-sixth year of my life I arrived at the lowest point of my vitality — I still lived, but without being able to see three paces in front of me. At that time — it was 1879 — I relinquished my Basel professorship, lived through the summer like a shadow in St. Moritz and the following winter, the most sunless of my life, *as* a shadow in Naumburg. . . . Even that filigree art of grasping and comprehending in general, that finger for nuances, that psychology of "looking around the corner" and whatever else characterizes me was learned only then, is the actual gift of that time in which everything in me became more subtle, observation itself together with all the organs of observation. To look from a morbid perspective towards *healthier* concepts and values, and again conversely to look down from the abundance and certainty of *rich* life into the secret labour of the instinct of *decadence* — that is what I have practiced most, it has been my own particular field of experience, in this, if in anything I am a master. I now have the skill and knowledge to *invert perspectives*: first reason why "revaluation of values" is perhaps possible at all to me alone. — (EH, 38, 39, 40)

So typical of Nietzsche, when he may have sensed his seriously declining powers — his energy, his abilities — to have devised something which he calls a "riddle," in order to obscure further what had become his controlling fascination. And any lover of his riddles is fascinated by the possibility of a solution.

To "tell myself my life" — he begins at the beginning. His fate, his "fatality," was that he was born of a father who was the village pastor (thirty-one years old), and a mother (only eighteen years old) who was the daughter of the village pastor of a nearby village. First born, this unique child, this male. His father died five years later, and his family then consisted of his mother, his paternal grandmother, his younger sister, and two maiden aunts.

"[A]s my father I have already died. . . . " Whatever his father had represented to him, whatever had been the young Nietzsche's perspectives on his father, whatever had been his profession, his person, his place in the family, his apparent weaknesses, Nietzsche rejected all of these. "[A]s my mother I still live and grow old." Whatever his young mother represented, whatever his own perspectives on his mother, her person, her place in the family, her apparent strengths (or weaknesses), Nietzsche was his mother's son.

We are always advised to pay careful attention to Nietzsche's every word. So listen more carefully to the description of his father — "My father died at the age of thirty-six: he was delicate, lovable, and morbid, like a being destined to pay this world only a passing visit — a gracious reminder of life rather than life itself." He was delicate — weak, fragile. He was lovable — attracted the attention and love of his family, but more importantly he was loved and favored by God. He was morbid — susceptible to gloomy unwholesomeness, corrupted, unhealthy, interested in death and life after death, not this life. He embodied the Christian denial of life. Nietzsche does not describe his mother. He had been born of this female, this woman, this mother and this male, this man, this father — this basic pair of opposites. Nietzsche leaves it to the reader to become the unriddler of his riddle. His mother is the antithesis, the direct opposite, in relation to his father. He had died; she was still living. He was delicate, weak; she was hearty, vigorous, strong. He was lovable, in particular he was loved and favored by God; she less so. His father was morbid, corrupted, unhealthy, interested in death and life after death, not this life. His mother embraced life, was enthusiastic, vigorous — she affirmed *this* life.

And remember:

> [M]y mother read to me: Gogol, Lermontov, Bret Harte, M. Twain, E. A. Poe. If you do not yet know the latest book by Twain, The *Adventures of Tom Sawyer,* it would be a pleasure for me to make you a little present of it. . . . (*PN, 73*)

In addition to, or beyond, the Bible.

In 1879, when Nietzsche's life appeared to be seriously threatened by illness, he was able to change himself from accepting his father's perspectives on the world, on life, on himself to those of his mother. These words are crucial in understanding Nietzsche, his perspectives on strength and weakness, and on how these perspectives had been one significant contribution to his entire way of thinking — about the world, about life, and about oneself. Let's continue a little further:

Setting aside the fact that I am a decadent, I am also its antithesis. My proof of this is, among other things, that in combating my sick conditions I always instinctively chose the right means: while the decadent as such always chooses the means harmful to him. As *summa summarum* I was healthy, as corner, as speciality I was *decadent*. That energy for absolute isolation and detachment from my accustomed circumstances, the way I compelled myself no longer to let myself be cared for, served, *doctored* — this betrayed an unconditional certainty of instinct as to *what* at that time was needful above all else. I took myself in hand, I myself made myself healthy again: the precondition for this — every physiologist will admit it — is that one is *fundamentally healthy*. A being who is typically morbid cannot become healthy, still less can he make himself healthy; conversely, for one who is typically healthy being sick can even be an energetic *stimulant* to life, to more life. Thus in fact does that long period of sickness seem to me *now*: I discovered life as it were anew, myself included, I tasted all good and even petty things in a way that others could not easily taste them — I made out of my will to health, to *life*, my philosophy! (*EH*, 40)

It is always exciting, and necessary, to listen carefully to Nietzsche's words, and none more than these words of what was probably his last book. Remember — he says, "How One Becomes What One Is." It seems puzzling, perhaps, that he uses the pronoun "what" rather than the pronoun "who." But then he says, "[I]t seems to me indispensable to say *who I am*." And the word is "who." One guess as to the solution to his riddle is this. "Who" is the person — the body that was given life by his mother. He is this human creature — this male. The remainder of the book is a short review of "what" he had become. He is "wise"; he is "clever"; he "writes good books" (and he reflects on some of the important ones); and he is "a destiny." He calls himself these and many others, and he says how he sees what he is not. Others might see him and call him many things. "Who" he is remains throughout his life — this male, with the name given him by his parents. As to "what" he is, or has become — indefinite numbers, different things, frequently changing.

What a paradigm for addressing the question of human *identity* and its relation to *power*. One is both creature and creator. One's natural identity is the body — male body or female body — and the basic physiology is the essential factor of an identity that remains the same throughout one's life. It is the basis of all perspectives, all experiences, all changes. One's capabilities, possibilities, abilities, impossibilities are all defined ultimately by the grounding of sex or gender. So each individual is a unity of the opposites same and different, just as female and male is a unity of same and different. Except, the sex that one is, is the original basis of one's identity.

There are other factors — ethnicity, which may be called part of one's natural identity, according to common racial, national, tribal, religious, linguistic, or cultural origin or background. However, ultimately all of these are properly applied to either male bodies or female bodies. Universally and necessarily the world, and every culture, exhibits this "uncanny dualism." Identity is "who" you are plus "what" you become. The terms female or male are always the modified, everything else is modifier. "He" or "she" may be, or become, many things or be called many things, but always remain, physiologically, "he" or "she."

Nietzsche, the artist said it this way:

> *One thing is needful.* — To "give style" to one's character — a great and rare art! It is practiced by those who survey all the strengths and weaknesses of their nature and then fit them into an artistic plan until every one of them appears as art and reason and even weaknesses delight the eye. Here a large mass of second nature has been added; there a piece of original nature has been removed — both times through long practice and daily work at it. Here the ugly that could not be removed is concealed; there it has been reinterpreted and made sublime. Much that is vague and resisted shaping has been saved and exploited for distant views; it is meant to beckon toward the far and immeasurable. In the end, when the work is finished, it becomes evident how the constraint of a single taste governed and formed everything large and small. Whether this taste was good or bad is less important than one might suppose, if only it was a single taste!. . . . For one thing is needful: that a human being should attain satisfaction with himself, whether it be by means of this or that poetry and art; only then is a human being at all tolerable to behold. Whoever is dissatisfied with himself is continually ready for revenge, and we others will be his victims, if only by having to endure his ugly sight. For the sight of what is ugly makes one bad and gloomy. (*GS*, 232, 233)

Create "what" you become, or are — best if accomplished by one person, one "taste," you yourself. You — *this* male or *this* female — to begin with, that's *who* you are. When Nietzsche affirms the principle "Amor Fati," the crucial center is your sexual body. Everything else is a function of, additions to, variations on, that.

In developing these ideas around the concept of power, it is beginning to appear that identity may be organically revealing itself as the most eye-catching. The questions — who am I? who are you? who exercises power? who defines power? who creates values? whose perspectives? whose interpretations? whose words? whose values? So, let's continue further.

In the first part of this book it was pointed out that one important idea that captured the attention and imagination of thinkers and writers of different persuasions during Nietzsche's lifetime was consciousness. That is, the acute awareness of, interest in, concern with, especially one's own experience, or experiences. And I wrote this:

> This interest in consciousness quickly expanded into species consciousness, class consciousness, race consciousness, gender or sexual consciousness, national consciousness, and historical or time consciousness. This usually included the growing awareness of, interest in, concern with one's own biological, or social or economic *rank* in society, a feeling of identification with those belonging to the same group or class as oneself.

> Charles Darwin's theory relating to species consciousness and Karl Marx's theory relating to class consciousness, along with the interest of both in historical consciousness — historical development or historical evolution — were already beginning to shake the traditional foundations of the West, especially the Christian religious base. Nietzsche was not unaware of the potential for conflict involved with each of these modes of consciousness. His own emerging or evolving concern, however, was not primarily at least, with species, class, race, or nationality, but rather with sexual or gender consciousness and with historical consciousness, as the latter opened up new possibilities for understanding the former.

Though not ignoring other types, Nietzsche's focus was clearly on sex or gender consciousness. And importantly, he claimed that rank was not inherent in the universe. For example, and particularly, there are males and there are females, but any notion of ranking is a human device, a procedure or plan, relating to the exercise, expression, or acquisition of power. Ranking is a major way of imposing order, arranging, organizing — what is called "hierarchy." It is creating a pattern in which each member is subordinate to the one above. It may be based on ability, or position, or something else. We speak of hierarchies of needs, of commands, of values — of most everything. In Nietzsche's thinking, as with everything, it is always about power.

And what about identity? As consciousness of oneself was emerging, perhaps the perspectives were on one type, or a few types. They were individual, and relatively simple. Today we appear to be overwhelmed by the complexities of possible identities, and by the pace at which this awareness has occurred, and is occurring. We perceive, and are conscious of, ourselves — and are perceived by others — as members of many groups, simultaneously. Species, race, economic class, social class, nationality, ethnicity, military, professional, political, age. And especially, religious and sex or gender. There are conflicts within each group, as well as among these groups.

Each one of these deserves a quick look. Here are some. Species — the controversy between advocates of evolutionary biology and those of religious creationism remains heated. Race — some people still ask "what is it"? or "what does it mean"? Nevertheless, the significance and power of race, or racial identity, in the contemporary world is growing. Socio-economic class — technology is fast bringing shocking images of the extent and severity of these differences around the globe. Nationality — again taking global perspectives, focus on any of the five most populated continents, particularly during the twentieth and so far the twenty-first centuries. Take your pick. Ethnicity — unfathomable, devastating clashes within, between, and among cultures. Military — which nation is the most powerful, and what does that mean, or imply? Which war? Who invents war? Who kills and is killed? Who or what justifies it? In no part of any society do the questions surrounding "who" proliferate faster and more ominously. No part equals the military in exhibiting and celebrating the power generated in hierarchies — the uses and abuses of power. In the military, identity is reduced to name, rank, and serial number — all of which could be otherwise. Politics — in the current world of politics all of these others appear to be in play. And religion — Nietzsche believed that one's religious identity had been for many centuries, and remained, the most powerful, the most easily accessible, the most widespread and enduring, the most dangerous. And he believed that the power exercised in persuading those less powerful of this identity had been instrumental in establishing the identity of gender, the ranking of the male as above the female — more valuable and more powerful.

The focus of this part of the interpretation of power is to consider briefly the possible ways in which power is integral to our identity — and perhaps also the reverse — in every instance of our life. Identity seems surprisingly and provocatively complex. There appear to be constantly shifting patterns, different emphases. We may speak of the politics of identity — the control, or manipulation, of one's identity — by oneself or by others. And the tactics. Consider for example, the proliferation of powerful symbols and images — of nationality, of race, of military, of politics, of religion — and of the body, or bodies.

One way of interpreting Nietzsche's thinking regarding identity is to say that being female or being male is a person's natural identity. All other senses of identity are subordinately natural or are cultural. It is "who" you are. It defines one's possibilities and impossibilities, one's capabilities and incapabilities, strengths and weaknesses. In spite of efforts to elevate other differences, other identities, above gender identity, all ultimately fail. If power and identity are inextricably related, and power and value are inextricably related, as Nietzsche claimed, then identity is inextricably related to one's value, and to one's values. Hobbes was suggesting something similar.

We are familiar today with identity theft, with false identity — pseudonyms, disguises, and the like. And, especially we want the ability to ascertain the identity of those whom we find threatening.

One final footnote — Nietzsche vehemently denounced his identity as German — his national identity — and adopted instead that of a "good European" — a good European male. And as a good European male, his perspectives on, and his interpretations of, his experiences with women almost surely were influenced by these situations or events. He was brought up within a family of women — mother, sister, grandmother, and aunts. He spent several years under the tutelage of the Swiss jurist and philologist, J. J. Bachofen. At the age of thirty-seven he saw the opera, *Carmen*, which became his favorite, and which, as has been suggested, became for him a counter of sorts to Wagner's operas. Soon after, he met Lou Salome, twenty-one year old Russian woman — whom he found most intelligent, highly entertaining, dedicated to her independence, and in his words, "an inspiration." He proposed, she refused — however, she was active intermittently during a good part of his remaining life. In *Ecce Homo*, reflecting on his writing of what he considered his masterpiece, *Thus Spoke Zarathustra*, Nietzsche wrote:

> The text, I may state expressly because a misunderstanding exists about it, is not by me: it is the astonishing inspiration of a young Russian lady with whom I was then friendly, Fraulein Lou von Salome. (*EH*, 100)

On the preceding page of the same book he wrote these words:

> The whole of Zarathustra might perhaps be reckoned as music; — certainly a rebirth of the art of *hearing* was a precondition of it. In a little mountain resort not far from Vincenza, Recoaro, where I spent the spring of the year 1881, I discovered together with my *maestro* and friend Peter Gast, who was likewise "reborn" that the phoenix music flew past us with lighter and more luminous wings than it had ever exhibited before. If on the other hand I reckon from that day forwards to the sudden delivery accomplished under the most improbable circumstances in February 1883 — the closing section, from which I have quoted a couple of sentences in the *Foreword*, was completed precisely at that sacred hour when Richard Wagner died in Venice — the pregnancy is seen to have lasted eighteen months. This term of precisely eighteen months might suggest, at least to Buddhists, that I am really a female elephant. — (*EH*, 99)

Chapter 18. Tactics

I suppose that in the continuing activity of the will to power in the drive or impulse to feel, to experience, to express or exercise power, to resist power — as the act of achieving a position of power which empowers oneself and may weaken, or empower, the other — there is always the semblance of a minimal strategy, or plan. And also there are tactics, devices for implementing the plan in accomplishing the end. Like many other things, there is an endless multiplicity of possible tactics. Here is an incomplete list, in no particular order: naming, framing, valuing, ranking, doubt, uncertainty, suspicion, exclusion, humiliation, deprivation, abandonment, rules, laws, ignorance, symbols, images, deception, lies, secrecy, interrogation, taboos, threats, silence, reward, punishment, fear, terror, physical force, torture, violence, kidnapping, obedience, war, justification, legitimation.

How to deal with these? It would be possible to give numerous examples, or instances, of any of them. Instead, as is frequently the case, Nietzsche suggests perhaps a model. It's worth quoting again, but in more length, what he wrote early in the development of his doctrine of the will to power:

> *On the doctrine of the feeling of power.* — Benefiting and hurting others are ways of exercising one's power over others; that is all one desires in such cases. One hurts those whom one wants to feel

one's power, for pain is a much more efficient means to that end than pleasure; pain always raises the question about its origin while pleasure is inclined to stop with itself without looking back. We benefit and show benevolence to those who are already dependent on us in some way (which means that they are used to thinking of us as causes); we want to increase their power because in that way we increase ours, or we want to show them how advantageous it is to be in our power; that way they will become more satisfied with their condition and more hostile to and willing to fight against the enemies of *our* power.

Whether benefiting or hurting others involves sacrifices for us does not affect the ultimate value of our actions. Even if we offer our lives, as martyrs do for their church, this is a sacrifice that is offered for *our* desire for power or for the purpose of preserving our feeling of power. Those who feel "I possess Truth" — how many possessions would they not abandon in order to save this feeling! What would they not throw overboard to stay "on top" — which means, *above* the others who lack "the Truth"!

Certainly the state in which we hurt others is rarely as agreeable, in an unadulterated way, as that in which we benefit others; it is a sign that we are still lacking power, or it shows a sense of frustration in the face of this poverty; it is accompanied by new dangers and uncertainties for what power we do possess, and clouds our horizon with the prospect of revenge, scorn, punishment and failure. (*GS*, 86, 87)

Nietzsche's major works were to follow in a short number of years. All of them were more extensive and deeper explorations into the complex nature and exercise of power. However, his early recognition of the oppositional exercise, or expression, of power may be a real ground upon which to understand Nietzsche better, as well as to grope further for a greater understanding of the convulsive character and enormities of power in our contemporary world. Only two ways of achieving the feeling of power — benefiting or hurting. He is speaking directly regarding others; however, the distinction is applicable to oneself — benefiting or harming oneself.

Certain terms lean heavily toward the side of hurting — fear, violence, horror, silence, ignorance, exclusion, taboos, threat, obedience, lies, or deception. Others incline in the direction of benefiting — protect, care, assist, praise, encourage, inspire, empower, applaud. And many more.

There obviously are an indefinite number of possible patterns consisting of plans, or strategies, and tactics, or means for achieving the end — the feeling of power. There are simple ones and complex ones; frequently used or widespread ones, and occasional ones; creative ones and destructive ones. But these patterns are never static, or in a state of equilibrium. They are in a continuing process of change, of becoming, shifting — always in motion. Variations of patterns, the pace of change, the momentum, the intensity — these constitute the *dynamics of power*. Think of the kaleidoscope, or better, ocean waves. Evolutionary change or revolutionary change — Nietzsche was clearly taking part in the latter and saw even greater changes ahead. Changes of authority and necessarily of values — his unfinished "revaluation of all values."

To create values was an extraordinary exercise of power. Read again Nietzsche's claim regarding "our best power":

> We who think and feel at the same time are those who really continually *fashion* something that had not been there before: the whole eternally growing world of valuations, colors, accents, perspectives, scales, affirmations, and negations. . . . Whatever has value in our world does not have value in itself, according to its nature — nature is always value-less, but has been given value at some time, as a present — and it was *we* who gave and bestowed it. Only we have created the world *that concerns man!* But precisely this knowledge we lack, and when we occasionally catch it for a fleeting moment we always forget it again immediately; we fail to recognize our best power and underestimate ourselves, the contemplatives, just a little. We are *neither as proud nor as happy* as we might be. (GS, 241, 242)

Who creates values? *Who* is valued and devalued, or revalued, in his "table of values" — for a "table of values" is the structuring principle of every culture. Which activities are valued? What things? Values, too, are constantly in flux, in conflict, but necessary and universal.

CHAPTER 19. REASON AND REASONS

When Nietzsche spoke about himself he said this:

> Every deep thinker fears being understood more than he fears being misunderstood. His vanity may suffer from the latter, but his heart, his fellow-feeling suffers from the former. (*BGE*, 230)

Also, remember he said these words:

> Everything deep loves masks; the deepest things have a veritable hatred of image and likeness. Might not *contrariety* be the only proper disguise to clothe the modesty of a god? A question worth asking. It would be surprising if some mystic hadn't at some time ventured upon it. There are events of such delicate nature that one would do well to bury them in gruffness and make them unrecognizable. . . . Such a concealed one, who instinctively uses speech for silence and withholding, and whose excuses for not communicating are inexhaustible, *wants* and encourages a mask of himself to wander about in the hearts and minds of his friends. And if he doesn't want it, one day his eyes will be opened to the fact that the mask is there anyway, and that it is good so. Every thinker needs a mask; even more, around every deep thinker a mask constantly grows, thanks to the continually wrong, i.e. superficial, interpretation of his every word, his every step, his every sign of life. — (*BGE*, 46, 47)

Nietzsche needed a mask. In our pursuit of the issue of reason — and in Nietzsche's view, the necessary relation of reason to power — the morass, the marshy ground, suggests that in addition to a dictionary, we may need boots.

What are some possible meanings of the word? First, as a verb, one finds these: to think or argue in a logical manner; to form conclusions, judgments, or inferences from facts of premises; to urge reasons which should determine belief of action; to think through logically; to conclude or infer; to convince, persuade, etc. by reasoning , e.g. to believe or act; to support with reasons. Then consider the word "reason" as a noun: an ability; a power of the mind, e.g., memory, speech; an inherent capability of the body, e.g. sight, sound; exceptional ability or aptitude. Synonyms include purpose, end, aim, objective. Also, capacity, aptitude, potential.

In philosophy, reason had traditionally been considered as the faculty, or power, of acquiring intellectual knowledge, either by direct understanding of first principles or by argument; or, the power of intelligent and dispassionate thought or of conduct influenced by such thought. As has been pointed out many times in this book, Nietzsche was a revolutionary. Most, perhaps all, ways of looking at, understanding, acting in the world, the nature of the self, were not only challenged but shattered. His "dynamite" was in placing power at the center of all thinking. Everything — reason, passions, all human activities — was related to, found its meaning in relation to, power. It was Nietzsche's "Copernican Revolution."

Importantly, he repositioned reason. He rejected Immanuel Kant's identification of something called "Pure Reason." At times Nietzsche referred to Kant as "Old Tartuffery," "comedian," "pretender," especially "pretender to piety." Nietzsche was critical of G.W.F. Hegel and the so-called "Hegelian Dialectic." Considering the activity of thinking as purely a logical process, as far as Nietzsche was concerned, might be of interest. But as with Kant, it remained disconnected with the world as Nietzsche was interpreting it. Any notion of reason, the activity of thinking, as being disinterested, for its own sake, for comprehension — Nietzsche would have none of that. The activity, or activities, of thinking , as with all other human activities, could be understood only in relation to power — the human will to power. Philosophical thinking, scientific thinking — these were never disinterested.

In reconsidering the function, or functions of reason, it appears that Nietzsche was very much influenced by Kant's identification of "Practical Reason." In Kant's view, reason could be exercised, and applied to, the problem of action, and choice, especially in ethical matters. Importantly, Kant recognized the ability to adopt means to an end. In Nietzsche's view, the function, or activity, of reason is always practical. It always is concerned with means to the end — the end being to achieve, maintain, and enhance the feeling of power. Reason involves the ability, i.e. power, and activity of planning — inventing or creating a strategy — and choosing the means, or tactics. The end itself is neither good nor bad — it simply is the basic nature of all living beings — necessary and universal. Nature — the natural world, and our sense experiences of that world — is, for Nietzsche, the source of all ideas. Just as energy is the source of all motion. Nietzsche, much like the Pre-Socratics, is a philosopher of Naturalism.

One important idea apparent in much of philosophical thinking, and again as far back as the Pre-Socratics, is that of synthesis, or synthesize. The term "synthesis" may mean "the composition or combination of parts or elements so as to form a whole." Synthesizing, of course, means to create a synthesis. The idea was extremely important in the philosophies of both Kant and Hegel. As for Nietzsche, he embraced the views of Heraclitus. In nature we perceive the unity of opposites, pairs of opposites which are unified by interdependence. Heraclitus reported some of these, and he may or may not have spoken about males and females in a similar manner. However, Nietzsche continued to expand, if obscurely at times, on the idea that the primary "given" in nature is that one — and that it is universal and necessary.

The issue of the passions, which had tormented and confounded many philosophers, necessarily fit into Nietzsche's total pattern. They were powerful, and they related to power in other aspects. We may venture this. He did say that perhaps the passions are the only things which are experienced immediately and directly. Perhaps they are the initial response to perceived power — particularly the emotions of fear, anger, or envy. We have already seen how fundamental the passion of resentment was in Nietzsche's criticism of Christianity. Passion — and then reason follows.

Be reminded — Nietzsche had a very different interpretation of names, and of the activity of naming. Remember this:

> *Only as creators!* — This has given me the greatest trouble and still does: to realize that what things *are called* is incomparably more important than what they are. The reputation, name, and appearance, the usual measure and weight of a thing, what it counts for — originally almost always wrong and arbitrary, thrown over things like a dress and altogether foreign to their nature and even to their skin — all this grows from generation unto generation, merely because people believe in it, until it gradually grows to be part of the thing and turns into it very body. What at first was appearance becomes in the end, almost invariably, the essence and is effective as such. How foolish it would be to suppose that one only needs to point out this origin and this misty shroud of delusion in order to *destroy* the world that counts for real, so-called *"reality."* We can destroy only as creators. — But let us not forget this either: it is enough to create new names and estimations and probabilities in order to create in the long run new "things." (*BGE*, 121, 122)

Naming or renaming, defining or redefining, interpreting or reinterpreting, are exercises of power, the power of words. Nietzsche named the universe — the "will to power." He renamed, redefined, reinterpreted morality:

> — morality understood as the doctrine of the rank-relations that produce the phenomenon we call "life." — (*BGE*, 22)

He redefined good, bad, and happiness:

> What is good? — All that heightens the feeling of power, the will to power, power itself in man. What is bad ? — All that proceeds from weakness. What is happiness? — The feeling that power *increases* — that a resistance is overcome. (*N*, 76)

And finally — Kant had wanted to make universalization the test of the rightness or wrongness of an action — the basis of an ethical judgment. Nietzsche rejected that and gave us, perhaps, a new and different basis — one that arises out of our own perceptions, interpretations, and evaluations. These words seem more basic and applicable the more frequently we listen to them:

> *On the doctrine of the feeling of power.* — Benefiting and hurting others are ways of exercising one's power over others; that is all one desires in such cases. (*GS*, 86)

Benefiting or hurting others, or oneself — quite a pair of contraries. And, as an addition to that, from the philosopher, who before Nietzsche or Kant, suggested the importance of a different psychological interpretation. A few selected excerpts from the writing of Thomas Hobbes will be beneficial:

> These small beginnings of motion within the body of man, before they appear in walking, speaking, striking, and other visible actions, are commonly called *endeavors*. This endeavor, when it is toward something which causes it, is called *appetite* or *desire*, the latter being the general name and the other oftentimes restrained to signify the desire for food, namely *hunger* and *thirst*. And when the endeavor is fromward something, it is generally called *aversion*. These words, *appetite* and *aversion*, we have from the Latins; and they both of them signify the motions, one of approaching, the other of retiring. For nature itself does often press upon men those truths which afterwards, when they look for somewhat beyond nature, they stumble at. For the Schools find in mere appetite to go or move no actual motion at all; but because some motion they must acknowledge, they call it metaphorical motion, which is but an absurd speech, for though words may be called metaphorical, bodies and motions cannot. . . . But whatsoever is the object of any man's appetite or desire, that is it which he for his part calls *good*; and the object of his hate and aversion, *evil*; and of his contempt, *vile* and *inconsiderable*. For these words good, evil, and contemptible, are ever used with relation to the person that uses them, there being nothing simply and absolutely so, nor any common rule of good and evil to be taken from the nature of the objects themselves — but from the person of the man, . . . And because the constitution of a man's body is in continual mutation, it is impossible that all the same things should always cause in him the same appetites and aversions; much less can all men consent in the desire of almost any one and the same object. (*AE*, 175)

First Hobbes and then Nietzsche recognized the subjectivity and relativity of assigning values — to individual persons, to human activities, and to things. Importantly, Hobbes early saw that individuals might psychologically be either attracted to, or have an aversion to, any person, any activity, any thing. He was discovering the power of these phenomena to attract or repel. His analysis claimed that these "psychological motions" varied among individuals, they were constantly changing, and implied that they were frequently in conflict for dominance.

As we know, Nietzsche was interested in the notion of "taste." These are some of his words:

> *Changed taste.* — The change in general taste is more powerful than that of opinions. Opinions, along with all proofs, refutations, and the whole intellectual masquerade, are merely symptoms of the change in taste and most certainly not what they are still often supposed to be, its causes.

> What changes the general taste? The fact that some individuals who are powerful and influential announce without any shame, *hoc est ridiculum, hoc est absurdum*, in short, the judgment of their taste and nausea; and then they enforce it tyranically. Thus they may coerce many, and gradually still more develop a new habit, and eventually *all* a new *need*. The reason why these individuals have different feelings and tastes is usually to be found in some oddity of their life style, nutrition, or digestion, perhaps a deficit or excess of inorganic salts in their blood and brain; in brief, in their *physis*. They have the courage to side with their *physis* and to heed its demands down to the subtlest nuances. Their aesthetic and moral judgments are among these "subtlest nuances" of the *physis*. (*GS*, 106, 107)

Physis is the Greek word for nature, and from many other comments, it surely meant for Nietzsche the physiology of the body.

Nietzsche indicated that the increasing rejection by some individuals of the messages, and especially of the moral values, of Christianity, was due not to opinions, but to *taste*. Increasingly, some individuals were not attracted to, but rather repulsed by, a morality, or order of values, that ranks the male — in power and value — over the female.

Nietzsche wrote this:

> *Against Christianity.* — What is now decisive against Christianity is our taste, no longer our reasons. (*GS*, 186)

Nietzsche's interest in taste as a philosophical issue almost certainly was stimulated by his reading of "Old Tartuffery" — Immanuel Kant — and Kant's way of dealing with the subject. A few brief comments on this most intriguing interpretation seems to attract. Kant was interested in the nature of the unity of the opposites, male and female, especially of course, within marriage. He did have a different, and creative, notion of the nature of that unity, that being complementarity. Together, male and female form a "single moral person." The male contributes rationality and learning; the female contributes taste and pleasantry. Kant admonished women against the pursuit of learning, which he counseled would weaken their charm — their ability to attract men. Man lives by reason, women by feeling. (*IW*, 127, 128)

Elaborating on the notion of taste, here are a few examples of Kant's comparison of the male and female, the masculine and the feminine:

> Women have a strong inborn feeling for all that is beautiful, elegant, and decorated. (*IW*, 130)

> The fair sex has just as much understanding as the male, but it is *beautiful understanding*, whereas ours should be a *deep understanding*, an expression that signifies identity with the sublime. (*IW*, 130, 131)

> Her philosophy is not to reason, but to sense. (*IW*, 132)

> Nothing is so much set against the beautiful as disgust, just as nothing sinks deeper beneath the sublime than the ridiculous. On this account no insult can be more painful to a man than being called a fool, and to a woman, than being called disgusting. (*IW*, 134)

> In such a relation then, a dispute over precedence is trifling and, where it occurs, is the surest sign of a coarse or dissimilarly matched taste. If it comes to such a state that the question is of the right of the superior to command, then the case is already utterly corrupted; . . . (*IW*, 144)

Back to Hobbes — perhaps Nietzsche, with his distinguishing between the extreme differences between benefiting and harming, plus Hobbes, with his distinguishing between attraction and aversion — together may have been forming a new philosophical and psychological basis for judging and acting. They both had their own ways of addressing the issues of power and values.

Typically, perhaps Nietzsche would advise experimenting with this possibility. Hobbes insisted that what he called appetite, or desire, and its opposite, aversion, were small beginnings of motion. That whatever is the object of any person's appetite or desire, it is that which one calls "good"; and whatever is the object of any person's aversion or hatred, it is that which one calls "evil." Hobbes further recognized that assigning value, or disvalue, to individual persons, to actions, or to things was relative to the person valuing the object. Nothing in the nature of the objects themselves were properly called good or evil. Objects have the power to attract or repel, but the valuing was a function of the person.

Nietzsche agreed — values were subjective and relative. And both agreed that the assigned values were constantly in flux. Nietzsche's interpretation was that in exercising the natural drive for power over others, a person may achieve power in only two ways — benefiting or hurting others. He does describe each way, and suggests that hurting others is "rarely as agreeable" as benefiting others — that is, from the perspective of the person exercising power.

But what about the perspectives — not of either the person exercising power or the person on whom the power is exercised — but of the observer of the action. If, as Hobbes thought, the object — in this case either the person exercising the power or the activity itself — had the power to attract or repel, the observer would call the person or the activity "good" or "evil." And either the person engaged in benefiting, or the activity of benefiting — or the person engaged in hurting, or the activity of hurting, could be called either "good" or "evil," depending on which was attractive or repulsive from the relative and subjective perspective of the observer.

Conceivably, more people might value, and call "good," exercising power in hurting others, or the reverse might prevail — calling "good" the exercising of power in benefiting others. *Who* is more attractive, more repulsive — the person benefiting others, or the person hurting others? Or the activity itself — benefiting or hurting?

If one believes as Nietzsche does, then harming others — planning by the use of reason and then choosing the tactics suitable to achieving the end, the feeling of power — may be understood as expressing a lack of power, a weakness, fraught with undesirable probable consequences. Remember — throughout Nietzsche's long and determined adventure in exploring the will to power, he never deviated from saying that power itself, or the discharge, the exercise, the expressing of power, was neither good nor bad. It simply was a given, natural, the essential nature of the world, of life itself, of every living organism. The possibility, the necessity, of judging the exercise of power, of valuing or disvaluing, must reside, not in the drive or impulse itself, but rather in the distinction of various ways of implementing or achieving that end.

Nietzsche also remained firm in his interpretation that values are the foundation of human cultures; that values are created by humans; that values are constantly changing; that the activity of creating, or destroying, values was itself an enormous exercising of power; and, that the values, which in his view, were to be given highest priority, were values assigned to persons, then to activities. There is no doubt that, in his view, "good" should be applied to persons who choose to pursue power, or the feeling of power, by benefiting, not harming others.

Borrowing from the Danish philosopher, Søren Kierkegaard, the few remaining comments could be called "Concluding Unscientific Postscripts." Nietzsche's thinking was so deep, so comprehensive, so utterly spell-binding, that we need to remember the breadth of the influences — philosophers, theologians, philologists, scientists, artists, and women.

Nietzsche's unfulfilled dream, the ultimate task which he finally set for himself, was the "revaluation of all values." It was a task which above all others was necessary, which must be undertaken following the demise of Christian values. The crucial fact remains that for Nietzsche value and power are inextricably related. And it is becoming more apparent that the important questions and issues concerning identity are related to power and values, intimately, if not inextricably. The task of the emerging new philosophers — "philosophers of the Perilous Perhaps" — according to Nietzsche, was to create new values. At the end of his brief life, he offered what was perhaps his own small beginning:

> The more a woman is a woman the more she defends herself tooth and nail against rights in general: for the state of nature, the eternal *war* between the sexes puts her in a superior position by far. — (*EH*, 76)

The "unriddling" of the riddle which is Nietzsche, the solving of the puzzle, is far from finished. Nietzsche was Dionysian. Some of us are Nietzschean. As for history, a new definition — history is the evolution of consciousness, of the continuing process, of the dynamics of power, between females and males. All else follows from that.

PART THREE

Chapter 20. The Experimenter

Part One of this book recognized Nietzsche particularly as a scientific philosopher, a classical philologist, a physiological psychologist, a poet, and a cultural historian and critic. But it extended the description to the category of "thinker" — as that person who exercised to the fullest his powers, i.e., his abilities and energies, both creatively and destructively to condemn Christianity, especially Christian morality.

Part Two of the book focused on the task of examining and extending further our understanding of the phenomenon of power. The basis of this interpretation was the belief that the necessary elements for such an interpretation were provided by Nietzsche, either directly or indirectly.

Part Three changes the focus on Nietzsche, or adds to the ways of describing or "naming" him, with the possibility that we may better understand his thinking and his place in the Western intellectual tradition. Certain of his major ideas remain — power, values, nature, sexuality, morality.

First, call him what he called himself — an "experimenter." Remember, he is a "Philosopher of the Perilous Perhaps." The influence of the rapidly developing sciences on Nietzsche cannot be overstated.

Many of the ideas and attempts to establish a new and promising epistemological method were immediately welcomed. In his own words:

> *Truthfulness.* — I favor any *skepsis* to which I may reply: "Let us try it!" But I no longer wish to hear anything of all those things and questions that do not permit any experiment. This is the limit of my "truthfulness"; for there courage has lost its right. (*GS*, 115)

> *As interpreters of our experiences.* — One sort of honesty has been alien to all founders of religions and their kind: They have never made their experiences a matter of conscience for knowledge. "What did I really experience? What happened in me and around me at that time? Was my reason bright enough? Was my will opposed to all deceptions of the senses and bold in resisting the fantastic?" None of them has asked such questions, nor do any of our dear religious people ask even now. On the contrary, they thirst after things that *go against reason*, and they do not wish to make it too hard for themselves to satisfy it. So they experience "miracles" and "rebirths" and hear the voices of little angels! But we, we others who thirst after reason, are determined to scrutinize our experiences as severely as a scientific experiment — hour after hour, day after day. We ourselves wish to be our experiments and guinea pigs. (*GS*, 253)

> *In media vita.* — No, life has not disappointed me. On the contrary, I find it truer, more desirable and mysterious every year — ever since the day when the great liberator came to me: the idea that life could be an experiment of the seeker for knowledge — and not a duty, not a calamity, not trickery. — And knowledge itself: let it be something else for others; for example, a bed to rest on, or the way to such a bed, or a diversion, or a form of leisure — for me it is a world of dangers and victories in which heroic feelings, too, find places to dance and play. "*Life as a means to knowledge*" — with this principle in one's heart one can live not only boldly but even gaily, and laugh gaily, too. And who knows how to laugh anyway and live well if he does not first know a good deal about war and victory? (*GS*, 255)

> A new species of philosopher is coming up over the horizon. I risk baptizing them with a name that is not devoid of peril. As I read them (as they allow themselves to be read — for it is characteristic of their type that they wish to remain riddles in some sense), these philosophers of the future have a right (perhaps also a wrong!) to be called: *Experimenters*. This name is only an experiment, and if you will, a temptation. (*BGE*, 48)

Nietzsche created an image of future philosophers in his own image. He was himself a philosopher of the future. Contrary to philosophers of the past — in his view, dogmatic and non-historical — these new philosophers must be experimental and historical, with a keen sense of the present, the past, and the future.

Ideas, invented or discovered, were to be subjected to the same rigorous scrutiny, testing, evaluation, acceptance, or rejection as any or all other invented or discovered items. A large part of the difficulty with Nietzsche's own thinking is that he seriously and vigorously explored the possibilities of this experimental method with his own, admittedly, often radical ideas. And he would have others do likewise — whether his ideas, or their own. The prime example of Nietzsche's persuasion of both experimentation and his new notion of the will-to-power as the defining motive of all human activity, was his extensive consideration of very different and questionable examples of human actions.

Nietzsche was learning about experimentation and the exciting possibilities of this new approach to learning. He was grasping the unexplored significance of the method, the process. And, most exciting for him and for us, he became the experimenter.

CHAPTER 21. THE CONTRARIAN

In both Part One and Part Two of this book, no little attention and emphasis was given to the importance of the idea of contraries, or opposites, in Nietzsche's thinking. Like the idea of power, the idea of opposition is obvious throughout his writing. The universe appeared to him as his "monster of energy" and as pairs of opposites — everywhere.

In both parts of the book, I considered it important to address the issue of contraries by reproducing the same quotation. In order to take a somewhat different perspective, here it is again:

> Everything deep loves masks; the deepest things have a veritable hatred of image and likeness. Might not *contrariety* be the only proper disguise to clothe the modesty of a god? A question worth asking. It would be surprising if some mystic hadn't at some time ventured upon it. There are events of such delicate nature that one would do well to bury them in gruffness and make them unrecognizable. . . . Such a concealed one, who instinctively uses speech for silence and withholding, and whose excuses for not communicating are inexhaustible, *wants* and encourages a mask of himself to wander about in the hearts and minds of his friends. And if he doesn't want it, one day his eyes will be opened to the fact that the mask is there anyway, and that it is good so. Every thinker needs a mask; even more, around every deep thinker a mask constantly grows, thanks to the continually wrong, i.e. superficial, interpretations of his every word, his every step, his every sign of life. — (*BGE*, 46, 47)

Martin Heidegger's familiarity with Nietzsche's thinking resulted in his issuing this alert to possible interpreters and critics. One will never understand Nietzsche without realizing the importance to him of the idea of reversal. Yes, there are a mosaic of small, individual pieces, separate pairs of opposites, which together formed a picture, or pattern. But, perhaps Heidegger had more in mind. Reverse usually means to turn completely about in position or direction, the opposite direction. Or, invert, which was the word used by Nietzsche in *Ecce Homo*, when he claimed, "I now have the skill and knowledge, to *invert perspectives*: first reason why a "revaluation of values" is perhaps possible at all to me alone."

Not only did Nietzsche have experience of many of these pairs of contraries, for example hot and cold, sickness and wellness, night and day; not only did he explore and expand fully the importance of opposites; but more significantly, he himself became the opposition, the reversal, the inversion. He firmly and steadfastly took and maintained a position contrary to the major conventional ideas of his time. He became the "antithesis," the voice of the next stage of the history of the West — in direct and unequivocal opposition — determined at whatever cost to change the direction of Western culture.

Several of Nietzsche's so-called reversals are worth noting. Recall this:

> Every deep thinker fears being understood more than he fears being misunderstood. His vanity may suffer from the latter, but his heart, his fellow-feeling suffers from the former. (*BGE*, 230)

As well as, "You see, I do my best to be understood with difficulty."

Nietzsche speaks often about war and warriors, and peace. He recognized the "eternal recurrence of war and peace." He preferred, and advocated, short episodes of peace followed by longer, more sustained periods of war. But never doubt that in taking this position, he was not referring to armed hostile conflict between states or nations, between opposing forces, or for a particular end. The conflict to be encouraged, which was a necessity, was the conflict of ideas, the war of words. In this war, he was the fierce warrior, determined to ultimately prevail.

Ideas were not to be thought of as things to be bought and sold in the marketplace. Rather, they were to be fought for or defended.

Nietzsche rejected, or repositioned, the abstract in favor of the concrete; the universal in favor of the particular; the absolute in favor of the relative; the categorical, or unconditional, in favor of the hypothetical, or conditional; the impersonal in favor of the personal; the objective in favor of the subjective; being in favor of becoming; dogmatism in favor of experience, or experiment.

Of the many positions which he staked out in pursuit of his mission, Nietzsche concentrated his power on the most formidable, the most well-fortified ideas — the ideology of values. He rejected nothing so vehemently as that which he considered the basis of any culture — the structure or ordering of values. Any culture is built and sustained upon those persons, those activities, those things, considered in terms of their relative worth, utility, or importance — the "table of values."

Of values in general, recall this from Nietzsche:

> We who think and feel at the same time are those who really continually *fashion* something that had not been there before: the whole eternally growing world of valuations, colors, accents, perspectives, scales, affirmations, and negations. . . . Whatever has value in our world does not have value in itself, according to its nature — nature is always value-less, but has been given value at some time, as a present — and it was *we* who gave and bestowed it. Only we have created the world *that concerns man!* But precisely this knowledge we lack, and when we occasionally catch it for a fleeting moment we always forget it again immediately; we fail to recognize our best power and underestimate ourselves, the contemplatives, just a little. We are *neither as proud nor as happy* as we might be. (*GS*, 241, 242)

This reversal, this change of position or direction involving values, was probably the most awe-inspiring, the most threatening within his arsenal. He decried what he saw as the devaluation of the natural world in favor of the idea of some other supernatural ideal world; the devaluation of this present life in favor of the idea of some other ideal life; the devaluation of sexuality and the human bodies — male and female — in favor of the idea of an immaterial, eternal soul.

Nietzsche increasingly, as his thinking developed, was obviously amazed, enchanted, puzzled, overwhelmed, by the apparent orderliness of the natural world — the dualistic structure. Opposites, contraries were everywhere. And he clearly adopted, and adapted, many of these for his own pleasure and power. But also, as with experimentation, he became the contrary, or contrarian — determined to vigorously oppose the ideas, and especially the values, of his own place and time.

CHAPTER 22. THE HISTORIAN

Given his studies both in philosophy and in classical philology, Nietzsche's interests and endeavors in history became a principal element in his thinking. He was familiar with the Greek historians, Xenophon, Herodotus, and Thucycides. He learned the philosophy of his German predecessor, Hegel. And, he spent several years under the influence of the Swiss jurist, philologist, social philosopher, and cultural historian, Bachofen.

In Part One of this book there is a discussion of some of the influence that may be attributed to Bachofen. Here is another lengthy quotation from the Introduction by Joseph Campbell to Bachofen's writings in *Myth, Religion, and Mother Right*:

> It is pertinent to remark at this point that in Bachofen's nineteenth century the Hegelian concept of a dialectic of statement and counterstatement, thesis and antithesis, in the rolling tide of history was a commonly accepted thought, inflected variously, however, by the numerous vigorous theorists of that really great period of creative historical thinkers. Karl Marx, for instance (whose dates, 1818–1883, match very closely those of our author), saw, wherever he looked, the economic-political conflict of exploiter and exploited. Nietzsche, who came to Basel in 1869 as a young professor of classical philology and for the next half decade was a frequent guest in Bachofen's home (spending Sundays, however, with his idol Richard Wagner in Lucerne, whose dates, 1813–1883, again approximately match Bachofen's span of

years), saw the dialectic of history, and of individual biography as well, in terms of an unrelenting conflict between the forces of disease, weakness, and life-resentment, on the one hand, and, on the other, courage and determination to build life forward toward a realization of potentials. Bachofen, far more learned in the matter of antiquity than either of these celebrated thinkers, and indeed than Hegel himself, saw the dialectic as of the mothering, feminine, earth-oriented, and the masculine, mastering, idea-and-heaven oriented powers. (MR, xlvi, xlvii)

It seems to me that reflections of many of Bachofen's ideas and interpretations are so evident and so important in Nietzsche's thinking, that it is difficult, if not impossible, to ignore the impact of these visits with Bachofen, the cultural historian. In the Preface to the same book, George Boas writes:

Bachofen's theory of a matriarchal society out of which modern patriarchal societies evolved was accepted pretty generally among sociologists until about the beginning of the twentieth century. It was the classic pattern for historians to follow. (MR, xviii)

Both Bachofen and Nietzsche took Western culture and the historical process which had eventually produced the nineteenth century, as the context of their interpretations. Neither was particularly interested in political, military, or economic events, past or present. Both found more compelling the evidence in intellectual, moral, aesthetic events — in religion, philosophy, language, art, science.

Bachofen appears to have thought in terms of some principle, or "law," governing the historical process. Referring to this as a "law" may have had its source in the fact that his profession was that of a jurist. Or, he may have been influenced by his own religious persuasion and the notion in the Old Testament of the law, or laws, of God. In any case, perhaps a word such as a recurring "pattern" might have served more appropriately.

Even so, the younger man clearly grasped the magnitude of the implications of Bachofen's new ways of thinking about history and culture. Nietzsche, as did Bachofen, began to perceive religion as the primary driving cultural instrument throughout the course of Western history. This interpretation of the power of religion, together with the dominating "pattern" within religious history being the dynamics of power between the sexes, I believe, plowed the fertile ground ready for Nietzsche's fertile imagination. Add to these new ideas the fact that Bachofen's work, while initially widely accepted and acclaimed, had during Nietzsche's lifetime been ridiculed and sometimes rejected. It suggests that Nietzsche was aware that the direction in which his own thinking was rapidly moving was inevitably leading to much greater rejection and condemnation. He had no doubt of the enormity of the threats which he was compiling, of the dangers to his own culture, and of his own perilous position.

Part One of this book began by pointing to Nietzsche's own judgment and design, his own keen unerring sense of his own time. Again, recall these words:

> Every deep thinker fears being understood more than he fears being misunderstood. His vanity may suffer from the latter, but his heart, his fellow-feeling suffers from the former. (*BGE*, 230)

And this which was said about him:

> [Y]ou have driven your artillery on the highest mountain, you have such guns as have never yet existed, and you need only shoot blindly to inspire terror all around. . . . (*PN*, 464)

In Part One of this book, suggesting a few special ideas which during Nietzsche's adult life were drawing the attention of thinkers and writers in many areas of study, I noted the following:

> Another closely related major idea, with expanding and possible future significance, was the idea of *consciousness*; that is, acute awareness of, interest in, concern with, especially one's own experience or experiences. This interest in consciousness quickly expanded into species consciousness, class consciousness, race consciousness, gender or sexual consciousness, national consciousness, and historical or time consciousness. This usually included the growing awareness of, interest in, concern with one's own biological, or social or economic *rank* in society, a feeling of identification with those belonging to the same group or class as oneself.

> Charles Darwin's theory relating to species consciousness and Karl Marx's theory relating to class consciousness, along with the interest of both in historical consciousness — historical development or historical evolution — were already beginning to shake the traditional foundations of the West, especially the Christian religious base. Nietzsche was not unaware of the potential for conflict involved with each of these modes of consciousness. His own emerging or evolving concern, however, was not primarily at least, with species, class, race, or nationality, but rather with sexual or gender consciousness and with historical conscious-

ness, as the latter opened up new possibilities for understanding the former.

It would be difficult not to assume that the historical conscious-ness of Nietzsche far exceeded that of any of his contemporaries — or even of those who followed after him. He learned, and was signifi-cantly influenced by, Hegel's theory of history. But much more intrigu-ing and provocative would be this claim. Nietzsche actually assumed a character and mantle from Hegel's metaphysical interpretation. He became Hegel's "World Historical Individual" on the stage of history. Nietzsche became a major actor in Western history, perhaps ultimately in world history. As Hegel had drawn the "World Historical Individu-al," Nietzsche had the insight to understand what he believed his own age needed and demanded — desperately. This was his "timeliness." His "untimeliness" was his recognition that his new ways of thinking were too dangerous, too revolutionary, to be "heard." He must wait un-til a later time. Remember, he said, "Some are born posthumously."

For Nietzsche, not history in the abstract, but history as he was living it, thinking it, writing it. And naturally, living his present meant also re-thinking the past and predicting the future — separate periods, but forming a continuing process. Nietzsche was/is the "brainchild" of both Bachofen and Hegel. He was a product of his own creative imagination.

In next to the last chapter of one of Nietzsche's last books, written in the last year of his life before his collapse, he wrote:

> Have I been understood? — I have not just now said a word that I could not have said five years ago through the mouth of Zarathustra. — The *unmasking* of Christian morality is an event without equal, a real catastrophe. He who exposes it is a *force majeure*, a destiny — he breaks the history of mankind into two parts. One lives *before* him, one lives *after* him. . . . (*EH*, 133)

One of the major recurring signature themes of Nietzsche's voice was that of morality, specifically Christian morality — which he be-lieved had been carefully, consistently, and successfully concealed for centuries. His definition of morality, itself cleverly partially concealed in another book, *Beyond Good and Evil*, needs to be repeated:

> This is why a philosopher should consider himself justified in including willing within the general sphere of morality — moral-

ity understood as the doctrine of rank-relations that produce the phenomenon we call "life." — (*BGE*, 21, 22)

Although having been concealed as the basis of the Christian religion, this morality has "hung over mankind as law, as categorical imperative!" Morality — the ranking of the sexes — was determined by, and determines, the "quanta of power, and nothing else. . . ." This morality, in Nietzsche's view, had been the instrument to maintain an order of power, of value, and of rank between males and females — past and present.

And how did Nietzsche view the future? Remember this:

> Every deep thinker needs a mask, even more, around every deep thinker a mask constantly grows, thanks to the continually wrong, i.e. superficial interpretations of his every word, his every step, his every sign of life. — (*BGE*, 47)

And in that remarkable final chapter of *Ecce Homo*, he begins:

> I know my fate. One day there will be associated with my name the recollection of something frightful — of a crisis like no other before on earth, of the profoundest collision of conscience, of a decision evoked *against* everything that until then had been believed in, demanded, sanctified. (*EH*, 126)

I think Nietzsche carried the weight of realizing the danger his thinking posed for his own time, and perhaps even greater the danger when perhaps he was better understood in the future — when he himself was *unmasked*. Could he possibly have foreseen anything comparable to the "convulsions" of the twentieth century, and continuing into the twenty-first century? Any interpretation of him leading to military power, without question, would have been an anathema to him — a curse, an obviously vain expression of the destructive power of men. Nietzsche became part of history.

CHAPTER 23. THE REVOLUTIONARY

If we want to establish the identity of Nietzsche, we know "who" he was. He was the first born, male, born 1844, of his parents — Karl Ludwig Nietzsche and Franziska Nietzsche. More significant to his identity was "what" he became during his forty-four years of activity — his history.

We have recognized him as a scientific philosopher, a classical philologist, a physiological psychologist, a poet, a cultural historian and critic, and of course, a thinker. We have added to those his having become an experimenter, a contrarian, and a historian (an active, pivotal character in history). And now to the most remarkable, enduring position among all the others — Nietzsche became a *revolutionary*. He was, to use his own phrase, "a continuator of the Renaissance," a period of vigorous artistic and intellectual activity, beginning in the fourteenth century in Italy, lasting into the seventeenth century. And he was situated in, and characterized by, the Zeitgeist — the general intellectual, moral, and cultural climate of his era — the spirit of revolution.

Relying on the dictionary, a reminder of the senses of revolution: the overthrow or repudiation and thorough replacement of an established government or political system; a radical and pervasive change in society and the social structure, especially one made suddenly and often accompanied by violence; a procedure or course, as if in a circuit, back to a starting point; rotation (Astron.), orbiting of one heavenly body around another; a round or cycle of events in time or a recurring period of time. Listening to Nietzsche over a long period, one can imagine that probably he would have embraced all of these meanings!

There was not just the sense or revolution or the spirit of revolution, it was a period of actual dramatic and far-reaching revolutions. The English Revolution (1688–1689), also called the Bloodless Revolution or the Glorious Revolution, expelled James II and conferred sovereignty on William and Mary. The American Revolution (1775–1783) won independence for the American colonies from Great Britain. The French Revolution (1789–1799) overthrew the absolute monarchy of the Bourbons and the system of aristocratic privilege, and ended with Napoleon's overthrow of the Directory and seizure of power. A little later in history the Russian Revolution (1917), also called the February Revolution and the October Revolution, saw the collapse of Czarist government, the establishment of a provisional government, followed by the overthrow of the provisional government and the establishment of the Soviet government. These political revolutions — always about power and the process of changing the relations of power.

There was another different, but similar, revolution. The Industrial Revolution involved a totality of changes in economic and social organization that began about 1760 in England and later in other countries, characterized chiefly by replacement of hand tools with power driven machines, and concentration of industry in large establishments 1840–1850).

And Nietzsche, the revolutionary? He called himself and his ideas "dynamite." He disguised himself with a mask, or masks. And he wrote this:

> Great men, like great ages, are explosives in which a tremendous force is stored up; their precondition is always historically and physiologically, that for a long time much has been gathered, stored up, saved up, and conserved for them — that there has been no explosion for a long time. Once the tension in the man has become too great, then the most accidental stimulus suffices to summon into the world the "genius," the "deed," the great destiny. What does the environment matter, then, or the age, or the "spirit of the age," or "public opinion"! (*PN*, 547)

And listen again to this:

> I know my fate. One day there will be associated with my name the recollection of something frightful — of a crisis like no other before on earth, of the profoundest collision of conscience, of a decision evoked *against* everything that until then had been believed in, demanded, sanctified. I am not a man. I am dynamite. — . . . I was the first to *discover* the truth, in that I was the first to sense — smell the lie as lie. . . . My genius is in my nostrils. . . . For when truth steps into battle with the lie of millennia we shall have convulsions, an earthquake spasm, a transposition of valley and mountain such as has never been dreamed of. The concept politics has then become completely absorbed into a war of spirits, all the power-structures of the old society have been blown into the air — they one and all reposed on the lie: there will be wars such as there have never yet been on earth.

Only after me will there be grand politics on earth. (*EH*, 126, 127)

The extent and intensity of Nietzsche's revolutionary pursuits were beyond political, economic, social, artistic, or intellectual. His intent was "astronomical," inconceivably large — a comprehensive cultural revolution, in particular, or beginning with, his own Western culture. Take a broad definition of culture: an integrated pattern of human knowledge, beliefs, behaviors, social forms, attitudes, values, goals, practices, tastes, that characterizes a group, and that depends upon man's capacity for learning and transmitting knowledge. Of all of the parts of this pattern, of any culture, the defining, activating, determining factor was, and is, values. Everything in the culture is shaped by, and reveals, its "table of values." And values have changed, are changing, and will continue to change in the future.

The ultimate purpose of Nietzsche's revolution was a "revaluation of all values" — a radically different and thoroughgoing "Copernican Revolution." To change a culture meant to change the values. And that meant, of course, a change in power relations. It was to this end that the genius — the extraordinary powers, especially as manifested in creative activities — of Nietzsche was committed.

Consider briefly these meanings of value, or values: of relative worth, merit, or importance; the ideals, customs, institutions, etc. of a society toward which the people of a group have an affectionate regard; force, significance (e.g. the value of a word); to calculate the monetary value of; to assess or appraise; to consider with respect to worth, excellence, usefulness, or importance; to regard or esteem highly; quality of, or in a person, action, or thing that entitles recognition.

As mentioned earlier, in Part One of this book, Thomas Hobbes apparently was the first philosopher to explicitly and in some detail connect the *person* with *value*, with *power*. And in his interpretation, he appears to have specified the sense of value as "to calculate the monetary value of." When speaking of power and value, this is what he wrote:

> The value or worth of a man is, as of all other things, his price — that is to say, so much as would be given for the use of his power — and therefore is not absolute but a thing dependent on the need and judgment of another. An able conductor of soldiers is of great price in time of war present or imminent, but in peace not so. . . . A learned and incorrupt judge is much worth in time of peace, but not so much in war. And as in other things so in men, not the seller but the buyer determines the price. For let a man as most men do, rate themselves at the highest value they can, yet their true value is no more than it is esteemed by others. . . . *Worthiness* is a thing different from the worth or value of a man, and also from his merit or desert, and consists in a particular power or ability. . . . (*AE*, 178, 179)

It is reasonable to think that Nietzsche was probably influenced by Hobbes, but to recognize that Nietzsche had his own rendition. In some sense, he spent much of his time, energy, and abilities, in broadly expanding both ideas — power and values. It is probably the case that in the critical Nietzschean literature, more recognition and attention have been given to the idea of power than to that of value, or values. Although the two appear to be inextricably related, the evidence seems to confirm that ultimately it was values that haunted and preoccupied his thinking.

Remember, Hobbes, and more emphatically Nietzsche, both claimed that values are not intrinsic to objects. Individuals give value, or values, to things. According to Nietzsche, it is the primary way in which humans create the world "which concerns man." The sweep of values over a culture is immense. At the center of that system, what concerned Nietzsche the most were values as they are bestowed on a person, or persons. What quality, what trait or characteristic, what feature, entitles a person to recognition? What is the basis of, or signifies, value?

Prior to Nietzsche's wrestling with the problem, the focus of philosophers had been directed almost entirely on human actions, not on the persons themselves. Ethics, or morality, was concerned with principles or rules of right or wrong conduct — frequently with regard to sexual matters, i.e., chastity. The major immediate predecessor of Nietzsche addressing the issues of moral values was Kant. Nietzsche took a very different perspective. He challenged what he believed was the entire system of values as defined by Christianity, seeing Christian moral values as being the most malicious and destructive. More than right or wrong behavior, he changed the discussion and interpretation to good and bad, or good and evil.

In Nietzsche's interpretation the dominating question, or questions, were directed toward "who." Who has, or is given value, or higher value? Who creates, assigns, determines these values? On what grounds or basis? From *Beyond Good and Evil*, this:

> It is obvious that the moral value-characteristics are at first applied to *people* and only later in a transferred sense to *acts* (BGE, 203)

Nietzsche, the philosopher, as did other philosophers before him, considered values, especially moral values, or ethics, a major part of his investigations. In fact, for him moral values, or morality, was *the* major part. However, philosophical thinking after him would never be the same following his affirming that philosophy — to be credible — was required to become "scientific" and "historical." This, in effect, was central to his revolutionary endeavors.

Regarding values in general, we have repeated several times Nietzsche's claim that values never belong to something by nature, never are part of the constitution or essential character of a thing. People create values, and these are constantly changing, or being changed. This was in the context of his larger framework that embraced everything in the world as continuously in process, in change, in becoming. This was revolutionary. His introduction of the idea that all living things, including and especially humans — all life — was basically characterized by the drive for power, or the feeling of power. This was revolutionary. When he stated that power and value, or values, are inextricably related, this was doubly revolutionary.

The dominant figure to introduce historical thinking into philosophy was Hegel, with his theory of the dialectical process of history, published in 1832. Several major philosophers and scientists almost immediately began to interpret Hegel's metaphysical theory of historical process in ways applicable to their own interests and ideas. Darwin developed his theory of biological evolution. Marx directed his thinking to social, political, and economic historical development. The Danish philosopher and theologian, Søren Kierkegaard, was another, with his interpretation favoring the historical development of the individual. Bachofen's philological interests took him back into the evolution of human cultures. All of these appeared on the scene just a little before Nietzsche.

In my view, considering Nietzsche's background and interests, the influence on his revolutionary approach to the question of values owed the most to Bachofen. Bachofen, in his own theory, had certainly made religion, power, values, and sexuality the driving forces of the evolution of cultural history. As one would expect, Nietzsche adapted historical thinking to his own purposes — the aim of which was ultimately a "revaluation of all values."

Very briefly — for the notion of "revaluation" needs a great amount of further investigation — this, I believe, is Nietzsche's approach. It brings together a few of his own strands of thought. Remember from *Beyond Good and Evil*:

> What is astonishing about the religiosity of the ancient Greeks, is the lavish abundance of gratitude that radiates from it. Only a very distinguished type of human being stands in *that* relation to nature and to life. Later, when the rabble came to rule in Greece, *fear* choked out religion and prepared the way for Christianity. (BGE, 58)

The ancient Greeks developed a set of values — ideals, customs, institutions, relationships, etc. toward which members of the culture had an affectionate regard. They valued and celebrated nature, life, the body, sexuality, procreation. And it is plausible that Nietzsche did not, or could not, ignore the emphasis placed by Bachofen on the predominance of the woman, especially the mother and daughter, in these earliest known cultures. The beginning of the process of cultural history

— the first stage — was premised as a period of "valuation" — values of affirmation, of a joyful "yes," to everything about life — this life.

The next stage of history — the antithetical — was the subject of Nietzsche's attack. Christianity created values opposite to these earlier ones. The negation, the "devaluation" of nature, life, the body, sexuality, and the female, characterized the long second stage of history, which Nietzsche saw as a disaster, a corruption, a failure, a lie. His rebuke and assault on these negative values was the subject of Part One of this book.

Nietzsche wrote constantly about values, and decried bitterly concerning the values of his era, Christian values. Believing firmly that a new phase of valuation was emerging, he named this new stage. The major philosophical task, his mission, was "The Revaluation of All Values." In 1888 he decided to write a collection of four essays entitled *Revaluation of All Values*. Before his collapse a few months later, he completed only the first essay, *The Antichrist*.

A few of Nietzsche's words on the subject are called for. In *Twilight of the Idols*, he wrote:

> A *revaluation of all values*, this question mark, so black, so tremendous that it casts shadows upon the man who puts it down — such a destiny of a task compels one to run into the sun every moment to shake off a heavy, all-too-heavy seriousness. Every means is proper for this; every "case" a case of luck. (*PN*, 465)

From *The Antichrist*:

> The problem I thus pose is not what shall succeed mankind in the sequence of living beings (man is an *end*), but what type of man shall be *bred*, shall be *willed*, for being higher in value, worthier of life, more certain of a future. (*PN*, 570)

> Christianity has cheated us out of the harvest of ancient culture. (*PN*, 652)

> The Christian church has left nothing untouched by its corruption; it has turned every value into an un-value, every truth into a lie, . . . (*PN*, 655)

> I call Christianity the one great curse, the one great innermost corruption, the one great instinct of revenge, for which no means is poisonous, stealthy, subterranean, *small* enough — I call it the one immortal blemish on mankind.

And time is reckoned from the *dies nefastus* with which this calamity began — after the *first* day of Christianity! *Why not rather after its last day? After today?* Revaluation of all values! (PN, 656)

From *Ecce Homo*:

Have I been understood? — I have not just now said a word that I could not have said five years ago through the mouth of Zarathustra. — The *unmasking* of Christian morality is an event without equal, a real catastrophe. He who exposes it is a *force majeure*, a destiny — he breaks the history of mankind into two parts. One lives *before* him, one lives *after* him. . . . The lightning-bolt of truth struck precisely that which formerly stood highest: he who grasps *what* was then destroyed had better see whether he has anything at all left in his hands. Everything hitherto called "truth" is recognized as the most harmful, malicious, most subterranean form of the lie; the holy pretext of "improving" mankind as the cunning to *suck out* life itself and to make it anaemic. Morality as *vampirism*. . . .

He who unmasks morality has therewith unmasked the value-lessness of all values which are or have been believed in; he no longer sees in the most revered, even *canonized* types of man anything venerable, he sees in them the most fateful kind of abortion, fateful because they exercise *fascination*. . . . The concept "God" invented as the antithetical concept to life — everything harmful, noxious, slanderous, the whole mortal enmity against life brought into one terrible unity! The concept "the Beyond," "real world" invented so as to deprive of value the *only* world which exists — so as to leave over no goal, no reason, no task for our earthly reality! The concept "soul," "spirit," finally even "immortal soul," invented so as to despise the body, so as to make it sick — "holy" — so as to bring to all the things in life which deserve serious attention, the questions of nutriment, residence, cleanliness, weather, a horrifying frivolity! Instead of health "salvation of the soul" — which is to say a *folie circulaire* between spasms of atonement and redemption hysteria! The concept "sin" invented together with the instrument of torture which goes with it, the concept of "free will," so as to confuse the instincts, so as to make mistrust of the instincts into second nature! In the concept of the "selfless," of the "self-denying," the actual badge of *decadence*, being *lured* by the harmful, no longer being *able* to discover where one's advantage lies, self-destruction, made the sign of value in general, made "duty," "holiness," the "divine" in man! (*EH*, 133, 134)

Nietzsche is often referred to as a nihilist, or as an advocate of nihilism. He did believe that conditions — the values, in particular the moral values — were so obviously corrupting that destruction of these values was not only desirable, but necessary and inevitable. But, a new constructive and creative valuation must, and would emerge.

Nietzsche's threat was to the *primacy* of the male — to the state of being first in importance, order, value, power, rank — within the culture. And, especially, in his view, within the most powerful part of the culture, religion. Religious dogma and religious institutions had promoted, enshrined, and sanctified this primacy. Both theologians and "priestly types" had been the perpetrators of what Nietzsche believed was the "greatest crime against life" and he reserved his most vicious contempt for both groups. Here is one expression:

> Let us here leave the possibility open that it is not mankind which is degenerating but only that parasitic species of man, the *priest*, who with the aid of morality has lied himself up to being the determiner of mankind's values — who divines in Christian morality his means to power. . . . And that is in fact *my* insight: the teachers, the leaders of mankind, theologians included, have also one and all been *decadents*: *thence* the revaluation of all values into the inimical to life, *thence* morality. . . . *Definition of morality*: morality — the idiosyncrasy of *decadents* with the hidden intention of *revenging themselves on life* — *and* successfully. I set store by *this* definition. — (EH, 132, 133)

For a very large part of human history, Nietzsche believed, the Christian West had been essentially a male creation. Rules, laws, values, definitions, names, images — regarding power, sexuality, family, state, church, everything — had been projections and products of male privilege.

Nietzsche devoted, perhaps exhausted, his life — his energies, his abilities — to diagnosing what he believed was the disease or condition of our culture, to analyzing and interpreting the signs and symptoms, looking for the cause or nature of the situation. He identified what he thought was the cause, or source. And not merely diagnosed but demanded the extirpation of the poison — the doctrines of Christian values. Nietzsche became a revolutionary who anticipated, took the first steps of the "Revaluation of All Values" — the Nietzschean Revolution.

BIBLIOGRAPHY

Nietzsche's Writings

(cited in the text by the initials given in parentheses)

Human, All Too Human (HA), Translated by Marion Faber, with Stephen Le-hmann, Introduction and notes by Marion Faber (The University of Nebraska Press, 1984)

The Gay Science (GS), Translated, with Commentary by Walter Kaufmann (Vintage Books Edition, March 1974, Random House, Inc. 1974)

Thus Spoke Zarathustra (Z), Translated and with a Preface by Walter Kaufmann (The Viking Press, Inc., Compass Books Edition, 1966)

Beyond Good and Evil (BGE), Translated and with an Introduction by Mari-anne Cowan (Gateway Editions, Ltd., 1955)

Twilight of the Idols (PN), in *The Portable Nietzsche*, Selected and Translated, with an Introduction, Prefaces, and Notes, by Walter Kaufmann (The Viking Press, Inc., 1968)

The Antichrist (PN), in *The Portable Nietzsche*, Selected and Translated, with an Introduction, Preface, and Notes, by Walter Kaufmann (The Viking Press, Inc., 1968)

Ecce Homo (EH), Translated, with an Introduction and Notes, by R. J. Hol-lingdale, (Penguin Books, 1979)

The Portable Nietzsche (PN), Selected and Translated, with an Introduction, Prefaces, and Notes, by Walter Kaufmann (The Viking Press, Inc., 1968)

The Will to Power (WP), Translated by Walter Kaufmann and R. J. Hollingdale, Edited, with Commentary, by Walter Kaufmann (Vintage Books Edition, 1968, Random House, Inc.)

Related Works

Nietzsche (N), by R. J. Hollingdale (First published in 1973 by Routledge & Kegan Paul Ltd.)

Myth, Religion, & Mother Right (MR), selected writings of J. J. Bachofen, with a preface by George Boas and an introduction by Joseph Campbell (published in 1967 by Princeton University Press, First Princeton/Bollingen Paperback Printing, 1973)

What Is Called Thinking (CT), by Martin Heidegger, English translation (Harper & Row, Publishers, Inc., First Harper Torchbook edition published 1972)

Hesiod (H), translated by Richard Lattimore, (The University of Michigan 1959)

Approaches to Ethics (AE), Representative Selections from Classical Times to the Present, Edited by W. T. Jones, Frederick Sontag, Morton O. Beckner, Robert J. Fogelin, (Copyright 1977, 1969, 1962 by McGraw-Hill, Inc.)

Envy (E), A Theory of Social Behavior, by Helmut Schoeck, Translated from the German by Michael Glenny and Betty Ross, (Copyright 1966 by Helmut Schoeck, A Helen and Kurt Wolff Book, Harcourt, Brace & World, Inc., New York)

The Basic Works of Aristotle (WA), Edited and with an Introduction by Richard McKeon, (Copyright 1941, by Random House, Inc.)

History of Ideas on Woman (IW), A Source Book, by Rosemary Agonito, (Copyright 1977 by Rosemary Agonito, Perigee Books, published by G. P. Putnam's Sons, New York)

INDEX

INDEX